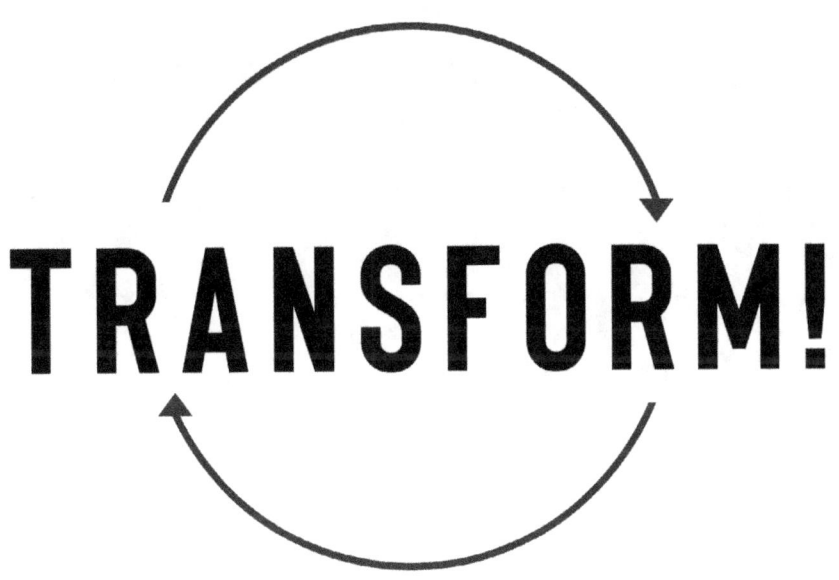

TRANSFORM!

**FREEDOM DEMANDS
PERSONAL TRANSFORMATION**

ARASH VOSSOUGHI

Published 2026 by Gildan Media LLC
aka G&D Media
www.GandDmedia.com

TRANSFORM. Copyright ©2026 by Voss Coaching Company, LLC. All rights reserved.

No part of this book may be used, reproduced or transmitted in any manner whatsoever, by any means (electronic, photocopying, recording, or otherwise), without the prior written permission of the author, except in the case of brief quotations embodied in critical articles and reviews. No liability is assumed with respect to the use of the information contained within. Although every precaution has been taken, the author and publisher assume no liability for errors or omissions. Neither is any liability assumed for damages resulting from the use of the information contained herein.

Front cover design by Amber Reed

Interior design by Meghan Day Healey of Story Horse, LLC

Library of Congress Cataloging-in-Publication Data is available upon request

ISBN: 978-1-7225-0697-1

10 9 8 7 6 5 4 3 2 1

Contents

Introduction: Transformation Is Not Optional   1

CHAPTER 1
Paint the Vision, Feel the Future
3

CHAPTER 2
Transformation Begins When You Decide What You Really Want
15

CHAPTER 3
Your Goal Must Become a Standard
27

CHAPTER 4
Programming: The Invisible Script Running Your Life
37

CHAPTER 5
Your Results Reflect Your Identity
51

CHAPTER 6
Identity Is a Daily Decision
59

CHAPTER 7
The Goal Achievement Process
67

CHAPTER 8
Discipline: The Key to Quantum Leaps
79

CHAPTER 9
Money Is a Mirror
85

CHAPTER 10
Don't Be Fooled by Circumstances
97

CHAPTER 11
Just Decide
109

CHAPTER 12
The Role of Environment in Your Transformation
121

CHAPTER 13
Mentorship: The Shortcut to Success
127

CHAPTER 14
The Power of Process
133

CHAPTER 15
Commit First, Solve Later: Trust the Process
141

A Final Word: Step into the Goal Achieved
147

Acknowledgments   157

About the Author   159

INTRODUCTION

Transformation Is Not Optional

I see you. I see you right there, diving into this book. You're probably tired. Tired of chasing, wishing, and grinding, tired of hoping for freedom but not seeing meaningful results.

You want to do something that fires you up and gives something back to the world.

I see that spark in you, that urge to transform your results and your life, and I truly believe in your ability to change.

How do I know all this? Because I was right where you are.

Not long ago, I was living a life that was the total opposite of where I am today. For three years, I was spinning my wheels. I felt I was doing everything right. I devoured hundreds of books, attended seminars, and watched videos, yet my results weren't budging until finally I had a breakthrough.

I've turned all my breakthroughs over the last two decades into specialized knowledge, and I've built this knowledge into a framework specifically to help you.

This book is about how you too can craft the personal freedom you dream of by transforming from the inside out. Through these pages, I'm here to guide you toward the best version of yourself.

You really can have it all. The key is willingness to let go of the old ideas, thoughts, and behaviors that haven't served you. It's about more than just learning new strategies. It's about fundamentally changing how you think and interact with the world every single day.

In each of the chapters ahead, I will walk you through specific frameworks and thought patterns that have led me, as well as countless others, to a life of freedom and fulfillment. We will tackle how to reshape your mindset, how to establish habits that are aligned with your goals, and how to maintain momentum even when challenges arise.

This isn't just theory. My framework is a practical, step-by-step blueprint that you can start applying right now to see real changes. If you're ready to leave behind what's been holding you back and step into a life of true freedom, let's get started.

CHAPTER 1

Paint the Vision, Feel the Future

About twenty years ago, I had been studying personal development for three years. At that time, I had read hundreds and hundreds of books. I would devour information wherever I could get it from seminars and videos.

Teacher after teacher and mentor after mentor told me to write out exactly how I wanted to live. Honestly, when I was writing, I didn't believe a word that I was putting on the sheet of paper.

One message started my transformation. One day a voice inside my head said, "Why don't you just do what you're being told?" So I wrote about an amazing vision—a vision in which I was financially free. I had more confidence than I ever had that I would end up being partners with visionary leader Bob Proctor.

At that time, Bob Proctor (who died in 2022) was a lecturer on New Thought and self-help, an author who was among the first to expound the law of attraction. I looked up to him, but I could not imagine how I was ever going to work with him. I didn't believe my own words, but writing the vision turned every word of that picture into reality.

That vision started to change my life. Months later, my wife encouraged me to go to Scottsdale, Arizona. Bob Proctor, was presenting. After the event was over, he was by himself in the seminar room, and my wife said, "Go take a picture with him."

I was reluctant and I said, "No, he's busy." But she kept nudging me to take a picture with him. I finally did, and as I was shaking his hand, I blurted out, "You and I will be working together very soon."

I don't know why I told him this, but it is exactly what happened. Less than six months later, he and I were working together. Not only was he mentoring me, he asked me to partner with him and be a part of his company.

For me, vision created opportunities. Now in this book, *Transform*, I intend to teach you how to earn more money, enjoy more freedom, and live the life you were destined to live.

In order to enjoy more freedom, it is crucial to earn more money. Living the life you are destined to live is your birthright. I want to encourage you, and as we go through this book, I'm going to teach you how to set big, ten-times-worthy goals.

A lot of people misunderstand what "ten times" is about. It is about setting goals that will lead you to an extraordinary life. But first, we have to embrace our current results. Embracing results is crucial. While most people bury their head in the sand and don't want to look at results, results always tell the story. The truth.

Number one, results give you clarity. Number two, they allow you to see positive patterns and negative patterns. Three, they prevent you from making the same mistakes over and over. Four, they show where you're excelling in your life, your business, your health, and your craft. Results emphasize what is most important to you.

Results Tell the Story

1. They give clarity.
2. They allow you to see both positive and negative patterns.
3. They prevent you from making the same mistakes over and over.
4. They show where you're excelling.

I want you to take a moment to look at your current results. What story are your current results telling you? What patterns are you seeing? What are the positive patterns and what are the negative patterns—the ones that you want to improve upon?

What knowledge are you picking up? What is the best thing you're currently doing? What is the most important step to help you take a quantum leap in your life?

Emotional maturity is crucial to transformation. Emotional maturity happens when you have a positive relationship with your past, regardless of the circumstances. We don't want to let the past go completely. We want to learn from it so we don't keep recreating it in our future. We want the past to be a university for ourselves.

Many people jump right into goal setting without looking and learning from their past, both positively and negatively. Yet your future can be found there.

When you're building a vision that is worthy of you, the most prominent question is, what do you want more than anything else? How do you really want to live? There is no vision without defining what you want.

What do you want more than anything else?
How do you really want to live?

What do you really want? My mentor asked me this question thousands of thousands of times in our fifteen years of working side by side. Bob Proctor would always ask, "Arash, what do you really want?"

Wants changed my life (I will get into this deeper in the coming chapters). But I had to understand how to bring my wants to the surface. What experiences would I like to have?

These critical questions brought my wants to the surface. I started thinking about how I could live instead of thinking about my limitations. What changes would I like to make?

Now I want you to ask these questions of yourself, because I want you to build a vision that is worthy of you—one that gives you so much juice, so much fire, so much inspiration, and so much excitement that you are willing to grow out of your comfort zone. These questions will be game changers in creating a vision that is worthy of you.

What do you really want?

What experiences would you like to have?

Let your imagination roll. Understand that life is about how we use our imagination and our mind. What experiences would you like to have? What changes would you like to make. Why are your goals so important to you?

This is the most important question: *what kind of person do I need to become to achieve all that I want?*

What kind of person do you need to become to achieve all that you want?

Many people fail to create the results that they want, not because they're incapable of it, but because they don't know who they are or what they want.

I want you to create a vision that makes you fall in love with your future, because you're creating your future in this present moment. What you're thinking about right now is creating your future. Make your future a magnificent obsession— a vision that is so inspiring, so exciting that you don't even have to think about it; it's always on your mind.

The present is meaningless unless you're connected to the future. The future dictates what decisions you make in this present moment; it drives your present. I'm going to share this message with you over and over again:

Most people are creating their vision from their past. I want you to create it regardless of what happened in your past.

If you live without a purpose, you are living in a prison. That describes 97 percent of the population. They are currently living in a prison that they don't even know about, because they haven't created a big future for themselves.

A purpose is essential to maintaining your vision, sticking to your purpose, and sustaining your faith and gratitude.

Once your vision is firmly grounded in your heart, it has to be accepted in your imagination; then it cannot fail to be realized. Goals are your vision of the future. Fall in love with the future. Design your life's masterpiece. Most people have fears of the future. If you're fearful of the future, you will be hiding and shrinking all the time.

I love sharing my mistakes. One of the biggest mistakes that kept me struggling was that I did not have a big vision, because I did not see myself bigger. I was living my life as an amateur. I was always shrinking and hiding and hesitating. Why? I was always worried about what people were thinking, so I was losing out on opportunity after opportunity. My back was against the wall, and I had no choice except to rise.

Now I don't want you to have to rise from as dire a situation as I was in. I want you to rise with every word of this book. The price is easy if you've made an irrevocable, committed decision. An irrevocable, committed decision is the death of everything opposite to that decision.

I want your decision right now to be that you are creating a world-class life. You are creating a life beyond your dreams, and you believe in yourself so much that you count on your ability to design your future.

Most people don't know how to create a vision. I'm going to show you how, just as I've shown thousands and thousands of clients in a hundred different countries.

Begin by getting into a quiet time. Put on some classical music, some Beethoven, some Mozart. Music of this kind will quiet your mind. I want you to write, in the present tense, the vision of how you are *already* living your ideal life, and I want you to do it for seven days because every day you're going to add to your written narrative. You're going to add to it and add to it.

Then recite your vision, record it, and listen to your words for ten minutes a day. This will implant that vision in your subconscious mind so that you accept it at your deepest level. I'll give you an example of a vision:

I'm so happy and grateful now that I am living the best version of my life. I am earning $100,000 or more every month doing what I love and loving what I do. My confidence has absolutely soared. I am consistently and constantly operating out of my comfort zone. I have a great inner circle that keeps stretching me. Every year I take four exotic vacations all over the world, and I'm experiencing many different cultures. Looking back over the last year, I'm blown away by how fast my life has transformed.

Before you start writing your vision, list every area of your life that you want to be a part of your vision, so you'll have cues. Write down words such as *health, spirituality, donation, finances, identity,* and *business*. Then you'll write about each area in the present tense.

The world you experience right now is nothing more than the ideas you have accepted on a deep subconscious level. Every success, every failure, every circumstance directly reflects what have you accepted as true in your consciousness. Most people fail at one key state: living from the wish fulfilled, from how they already want to live. They continue to live from their circumstances rather than from the state they desire to experience.

When you want something, whether it be wealth, health, success, or any other desire, you must first understand that it already exists.

When you want something, you must first understand that it already exists.

What is your *why*? We only do things because we have enough reason to do them. When our *why* is big enough, the *how* will show itself. When your *why* is big enough, you will break through barriers and limitations, and the way will show itself.

The secret lies not in working toward your vision, but in accepting that you already have it. This is where people stay stuck. They think their desires are somewhere in the future. The future is right now. Your future is created right in this moment, by what you're accepting.

People continue to stay in the state of wanting, which activates more lack in their lives. They declare to their own subconscious minds that success is outside of them. This assumption keeps them in the state of wanting.

Instead, you must assume that your wish has been fulfilled. You must go about your day feeling successful.

How would you feel if your vision were impossible to fail? That's how I want you to feel. I want you to think from success, act from success. This is a present fact. If you desire success, you must feel successful.

If you desire wealth, you must feel wealthy *now*. How do you feel successful and wealthy? I want you to imagine the level of success you want *right now*. What would it feel like if you had it? How excited would you feel? How proud would you feel? How much peace of mind would you have? That's what I want you to feel all day long. That's how you bring your vision into reality and how you bring your future into this present moment—right now.

When you persist in that belief, the power of your assumption becomes exactly what you experience. Most people live their entire lives never realizing that their imagination is actually the very substance of reality. They see imagination as only fantasy, as something separate from reality. The goal you wish to achieve already exists in your imagination. It is as real as anything you accept as fact. The only difference is your assumption about what is real and what is imagined.

You never attract what you *want*. You attract what you *are*. You are the ideas you constantly accept. Take a look at your results right now. They are the truest reflection of who you think you are on a deep, subconscious level.

**You never attract what you *want*.
You attract what you *are*.**

This is why affirmations don't work for most people. You cannot affirm externally what you deny internally.

Instead of working hard to achieve something, you must assume you already have it. I want you to assume the vision that you have written out is already yours. When you assume a state of being, you must persist in that state until it becomes your dominant feeling.

How is your vision going to become your dominant feeling? I want you to think of your vision as like breathing or brushing your teeth: it's just a part of what you do. When you brush your teeth, you don't wonder, "I've got to go with this angle to brush my teeth." Brushing your teeth is just what you do.

Get comfortable with the idea of success. This is where most people fail. They are always starting and stopping instead of persisting long enough.

You may think right now that your senses define your reality. Your senses are only showing you what your mindset has already accepted as true. Whatever you assume with complete conviction must be experienced in your results.

Most people visualize and then live from their current circumstances the rest of the day. Have you ever experienced that? I know I used to. They imagine themselves as wealthy for a moment, then they return to reacting to their current financial situation. This double-binding message prevents them from achieving their goals and dreams.

You must give your vision time to materialize. The seed must have time to grow. Your ideas are spiritual seeds. The time will always accord with how long it takes you to feel natural at your new frequency.

You must persist in your new state until it feels just as natural as your present results. When you emotionally realize that your results are an exact reflection of your consciousness, you will be off to the races. Your results will chase you, and you will never have to chase a result again.

Many people miss by failing to master their assumptions. Accepting and rejecting ideas is critical to success. Get into the practice of rejecting, within a millisecond, every thought that you have that is *not* aligned with your vision. With the same speed, accept every thought that *is* aligned with your vision. Our imagination immediately passes on the ideas we accept, either consciously or unconsciously, to our subconscious mind.

This principle is known as the *law of assumption*. You follow this law by accepting and rejecting ideas not *toward* your vision but *from* your vision. This practice will bring results into your physical experience at an astonishing rate.

Remember, your vision is already here. Creation is already finished. Your goals are already here. You just have to go to the frequency where they already exist. When following this consistently over sixty or ninety days, you are going to see your results come into your physical reality at an exponentially fast rate.

**Your vision is already here.
Creation is already finished.**

Every time you react to an event badly or talk negatively to yourself, you are setting in motion what you are speaking about. Every time you unconsciously speak and say something like, "I am broke. I am struggling," you're speaking what is true about you. Yet on a deep subconscious level, these are facts only because you have made them facts with your assumptions.

The secret of your success is manipulating your awareness from one state to another. You must assume the consciousness of the person you wish to be.

How do you train yourself to leverage your "I am" statements? Your self-talk has to be aligned with the vision you desire. In his great book *The Magic of Thinking Big*, David Schwartz states that we are speaking either our castles or our funerals into existence.

Now create ten "I am" statements that are aligned with your vision, such as:

- I am infinitely rich.
- I am infinitely healthy.

- I am infinitely abundant.
- I am prosperous.
- I am prosperity.
- I am powerful.

These are examples. *I am* are the two most important words in your vocabulary. The law works perfectly every time. Look at your current results. When you are winning, you are working in harmony with the law. When you are struggling, you are working against the law. Whatever you are being, you will attract for your vision to be fulfilled.

Faith is critical. Faith is not believing something will happen in the future; faith is accepting it as fact—feeling the results as already achieved even though your senses tell you otherwise. Your assumptions must be planted inside your subconscious mind and given time to grow. The results will only appear when you persist long enough in your assumptions.

You must assume the end result. Your actions, your attitudes, and your words must come from your vision of what you have already achieved. This is not easy—the evidence of your senses will constantly try to pull you back into your past or present self—but if practiced consistently, it becomes a new habit. This practice is crucial for achieving your vision. Persist and be faithful to your vision. Consistency always compounds. Consistency builds unstoppable momentum.

Key Points in This Chapter

- Paint a clear vision for your desired future. Live as if you have already achieved that vision rather than being limited by your current circumstances.
- Write out a detailed vision for your ideal life in the present tense. Read it aloud, record it, and listen to it daily to impress your vision upon your subconscious mind.
- Use the power of assumptions and beliefs to shape your reality. Reject any thoughts that are not aligned with your vision. Fully embody the state of having already achieved your goals.
- Consistent self-talk and "I am" statements reflect your vision. They are crucial for manifesting your desired future.
- Faith and persistence in your vision are essential, even when your senses tell you otherwise.
- The results will materialize when you continue to live as if you have already achieved the end results.

CHAPTER 2

Transformation Begins When You Decide What You Really Want

I first understood the importance of wants during a conversation with Bob Proctor. He asked me, "Arash, what do you really want?"

I said, "I'm not really sure."

To which he replied, "You have to know your want. Want starts everything in the creation process. Ninety-eight out of a hundred people have no idea what they want. It's not because they can't achieve it. I cannot help you unless you know what you want."

He was so stern that this conversation created an emotional impact.

As the conversation continued, I said, "I don't know exactly how I'm going to get there."

"You don't need to know the *how*. You just need to tell me what you want, and I will show you how to get there."

I had never spoken to anybody who was so confident and made it so simple. I said, "Bob, I would like a life of freedom. I am sick and tired of being sick and tired."

"So you do know what you want."

From that day on, I have always had a want because he imprinted on me the importance of a want.

I want to congratulate you for joining me in your transformational growth. Our personal growth is worth investing in. Just by reading this book, you are creating an identity shift. In the coming chapters, I want to teach you how to build, not just big ideas, but extraordinary ideas that will make you grow out of your comfort zone. Transformation creates personal freedom, but it demands that we work out of our comfort zone.

I want you to understand that big things are ahead for you. Everything that has happened in your life has been absolutely essential to prepare you for what you're about to accomplish. All the failures, all the successes, all the starting and stopping, all the setbacks, all the adversity, all the accolades—everything has prepared you right now for all the big things that are coming for you.

Simplicity scales; complexity fails.

Success always comes down to a few simple choices. I want you to remember this phrase: *simplicity scales; complexity fails*. The three choices are always, first, to decide exactly what you really want. Second, you have to determine the price you will have to pay. That price is upgrading your standards. That price is discipline. That price is working out of your comfort zone. That price is building an idea that's bigger than yourself. That price is upgrading your inner circle.

The third point is, you have to decide whether you are willing to pay the price.

Three Choices for Success

1. Decide exactly what you really want.
2. Determine the price you will have to pay.
3. Decide whether you are willing to pay the price.

During my twenty years of transforming people's lives in hundreds of countries, I've discovered that you are always paying the price. You are either paying the price of freedom or paying the price of regret. In either case, the price is always paid in full.

Transformation Begins When You Decide What...

Plant in your mind what you really want, and give yourself a second to really see what's coming up for you. Motivational speaker Eric Thomas famously said that you have to want success as badly as you want to breathe. The source is this story. Told about Socrates, it is apocryphal, but it illustrates the point remarkably well.

A young aspiring philosopher came to Socrates and said, "Socrates, I really want your help."

Socrates said, "Well, how can I help you?"

"I want to be as great of a philosopher as you."

Socrates took the young man to a lake and asked him to kneel down next to it. Socrates grabbed him by the neck, put his head in the water, and held it there—and then he finally pulled his head out.

"What were you thinking about?" he asked the man.

"All I wanted to do was breathe."

"If you want to be a great philosopher, you have to want it as badly as you want to breathe."

You have to want success as badly as you want to breathe. When your want is that strong, you will not wilt when adversity comes—because it will come.

You have to want success as badly as you want to breathe.

I want you right now to willingly suspend disbelief. Let go of all your doubts. Whatever you're doubting, doubt your doubts.

You might be thinking, "I've been wanting to improve my life for years, but it's never happened." Just because you couldn't do something last year doesn't mean that you can't master it this year. Were you as committed to transforming your life last year as you are this year?

In this book, I'm going to show you that transformation is your birthright. Transformation happens in moments when you decide to bet on yourself. It starts with making an irrevocable, committed decision—a decision where you are all in and by which you operate no matter what. Such an irrevocable decision opens the floodgates to creating a world-class life.

Nothing happens until you make a decision. I want you to decide right now to have the courage to bet on yourself. There is no one better to bet on than you.

A life of freedom is not a courage-free life. You have to keep upgrading your courage muscle at every level to get to. If you study the top 0.1 percent of individuals, you'll see that they have more courage now than they ever had. It's not about having a life that's beyond courage: it's about tapping into different levels of courage.

A few years ago, I was in Portofino, Italy, sitting on the balcony overlooking the ocean while my wife was getting ready for the day. This thought came over me: "What was it that you really did that turned your life from failing to succeeding?" Within a second, a voice said, "The minute you bet on yourself, everything started to work in your favor."

I want you to understand there's no one better to bet on than you because you have infinite potential within you. Your spiritual DNA is perfect. Courage is not a one-time act. Courage is betting on yourself. It is a decision that you'll have to do over and over again if you want to be successful and create a life of freedom.

> **Courage is not a one-time act.
> Courage is betting on yourself.**

Freedom was an extremely important word for me. After over twenty years of working with some of the top minds in the world, I have learned that everyone wants one thing: freedom. They want peace of mind.

Where you are currently in your life is in harmony with your past. Take an honest look at your present results. Right now, you can only attract what you are in harmony with every day. Our biggest enemy is our present results. We never want to make decisions from our present results: we want to make them from the future that we are creating in this very moment. Present results are a brick wall we run into every day. We're letting present results control our identity, our attitude, and our thinking.

Your wants are critical, but to commit to them, you have to release your hidden commitments.

There is something in your life right now that is a hidden commitment, which you think you can bring with you into the future.

I promise you, you can't.

Examples of hidden commitments are somebody who wants to scale their business but is never reaching out to clients, or somebody who wants to get in the best shape of their life, yet they are drinking and overeating.

Those are hidden commitments. What is your hidden commitment? Mine used to be always protecting myself from what I wanted.

Identify the hidden commitment that you're not willing to look at: you think you can create a big future without dealing with it. Decide right now to stop protecting yourself from who you really want to be, from the type of life you want to create.

> **Identify the hidden commitment that you're not willing to look at.**

Life becomes magical when you stop protecting yourself and you fall in love with who you really are. You right now are an amazing story. Ask yourself honestly: "Do I see myself as an amazing story?" Most people don't. Yet every person walking this planet is an amazing story. I want you to accept that idea right now. Everyone has greatness inside of them. You may not have brought it to the surface yet, because your awareness has not accepted that idea.

I can't give you greatness. But I can bring it out of you through this book, because greatness is inside of you, and we've got to let it out.

How do we let it out? We have to first understand that it is inside of us. For most people, greatness is covered up by a coat of worry, doubt, fear, and shame. Let that go. Give yourself a blank slate, whether you're winning big right now or whether you're struggling. What you do going forward is creating your future.

Greatness is misunderstood. Greatness is about attracting what you expect. Your expectations always control your behaviors. Greatness is about reflecting and leading by example and already being the desire you want to accomplish in your life. Greatness is about becoming what you respect and mirroring what you admire.

Committing to excellence means showing up and doing the work. The ideas in this book work for every single person, but only if you work them. To create your want, to do what it takes to become great, it is essential to understand the laws of your mind. Understanding the laws of your mind is essential for a life of freedom.

Understanding the laws of your mind is essential for a life of freedom.

Everything is about awareness. Look at your present results. They are what you're aware of. There are no limitations in the universe; there are only limitations in your awareness. An amazing, extraordinary inner world exists within all of us; understanding this world enables us to do and achieve anything we desire within the laws of the universe.

When I was first starting to work with Bob Proctor, he said, "Arash, there are only two things you need to know. You need to understand the laws of your mind and work in harmony with the laws of your mind, and you need to understand the laws of the universe and work in harmony with the laws of the universe."

"Bob," I said, "that doesn't seem like a lot."

Once you understand how your mind works and start working in harmony with it, magic is going to happen. When you get in harmony with the spiritual essence of who you are, floodgates will open for you. You are a spiritual being living in a physical body, yet most people are living only from the physical side of themselves. They're constantly letting the outside control them, and they don't tap into the genius inside of them.

Let me explain how your mind works. This point is so important that I don't want you to continue on with this chapter until you understand exactly what I am sharing with you.

Three Parts of the Mind

1. The conscious mind
2. The subconscious mind
3. The body

There are three parts to your mind. There's your *conscious mind*, your *subconscious mind*, and your *body*. Your *conscious mind* is your thinking mind. It's your educated mind. It's where your intellect resides. If you look at your results right now, they will tell you how you're using your intellect. Your intellect always creates your environment.

Your *subconscious mind* is your emotional mind. It is your powerhouse, Your conscious mind. You can choose whatever ideas you want. You can choose whatever thought you want. I want you to choose big ideas. I want your subconscious mind to see you as enormous. You can accept or reject any idea depending on whether it furthers that goal or detracts from it. Accepting or rejecting is the law of assumption.

This is how you build discipline: From this moment on, put your number one goal in your mind—what you want to achieve more than anything else. Accept anything that is in harmony with that goal, even though it is out of your comfort zone. Reject everything else.

Accepting and rejecting thoughts will change your life. The art and discipline of accepting or rejecting ideas creates your results. Whenever you accept an idea, it goes right into your imagination and right into your subconscious mind.

Accepting and rejecting thoughts will change your life.

I used to think that discipline was hard for me, because it used to be hard. I didn't understand what discipline was. I used to think it meant my activities. But discipline is thinking. Most people let the outside world discipline them, but a conscious person accepts and rejects ideas. That's what discipline is.

Try this test for thirty days: accept and reject ideas from your goal already achieved. Originate big ideas, because it takes just as much energy or effort to soar in life as it does to settle. Your subconscious mind must accept the ideas you supply to it. Whenever we fail to reject an idea that is harming us, we are automatically accepting it, and it is going right to our subconscious mind. Your subconscious mind has no ability to reject. It is impersonal. It doesn't know what's good for you or what's bad for you. It only gives you what you've given it, and it cannot determine the difference between what is real and what's imagined.

Whatever you put into your subconscious mind, your *body*, the third component of your mind, will experience as results. The intellect enables you to tap into your spiritual side and change your physical results. You want to bulletproof your intellect.

Let's get back to the main question: what do you really want more than anything else in the world? It's not just what you *kind* of want. What do you *really* want more than anything else in the world?

Never justify your wants to anybody. You own them; they are yours. Wants start in the subconscious mind: this is where your heart is. Your wants are then channeled to your conscious mind, which says, "This is the new idea." Your job is to accept it. Your wants create abundance.

Most people will get a big idea, get superjazzed about it, and then give up on it a day or an hour later, because they say, "I can't do that." They don't understand the laws of the mind. Everything you want is meant to be fulfilled unless you give up on it. That's the only way that it's *not* going to be fulfilled.

When you get a want, your job is to accept it. Tell yourself, "This is what I'm going to work at. This is how I'm going to live." But don't stay in the wanting state. Turn the idea back over to your subconscious mind through constant repetition until it becomes a desire. Once it's a desire, it's a done deal.

> Once it's a desire, it's a done deal.

A desire is a release of energy. It will alter your vibration: your conditions, circumstances, and environment will change, and your results will manifest in your life.

How do you get a want to become a desire? By the repetition of repeating a statement over and over to yourself and living the rest of your day from that statement.

Let me give you an example. Consider someone who wants to take their income from $100,000 a year to $100,000 a month. They really want to create a seven-figure income. I would instruct them (and I'm instructing you) to write a clear, concise, definite statement: *I am so happy and grateful that I am earning $100,000 or more every month, and I love it.*

Put an alarm on your phone to alert you every three hours. When the alarm goes off, I want you to get emotionally involved with that idea. How? You repeat the statement to yourself over and over again: *I am so happy and grateful that I am earning $100,000 or more every month, and I love it.* You repeat it for two minutes.

Then visualize for one minute what it would feel like if you already have this income. By repeating this exercise over a ninety-day period, your want will turn into a desire.

Another technique is to visualize for ten minutes a day that you are already experiencing your desire as fulfilled. Discipline your senses: See what you would see if you had already achieved what you desire. What would you be seeing with your physical eyes? What would you be hearing? What would you be smelling? Would people be congratulating you? Get into a relaxed state, close your eyes, and hear what they would be saying. Would you be at a celebratory dinner? What would you be feeling? Feel the excitement. Feel the joy. Feel the pride. Feel the peace of mind.

These two examples of autosuggestion show you how to plant your big idea in your subconscious mind. But your want will only manifest if you radically accept that idea. Radical acceptance puts it on steroids. It becomes the dominant idea that you are coming from all day long. You'll know that you've radically accepted an idea when you are never worried about the *how*; you're only focused on *who* you need to become. What are your highest income-producing activities? What are your highest health-producing activities?

You won't worry about the circumstances, because they are based on your past. Once you radically accept an idea, you have made your future your magnificent obsession. It is always on your mind. Once your want is an obsession, your desired goal turns into a love story.

Think about when you first fell in love. You didn't have to remind yourself to think about that person. Similarly, until your goal becomes a love story, where it's always on your mind, it will stay in the wanting state. Everything you want is on its own frequency. Faith is a frequency. Every thought is a frequency. Your job is to become one with the frequency of what you want.

The biggest way to sabotage the creation of what you want is to come from a place of neediness and focus your energy on your present results. Lack breeds more lack. Remind yourself: "My present results are created from the past. What I'm creating now is going to be much bigger and better."

The other way to sabotage the creation of what you want is focusing on what's missing. I want you to have the attitude of growth. Transformation is about growth. Growth is good for the soul. Never be satisfied, but always be grateful. Look for the good in everything, even in adversity. At the same time, understand that satisfaction creates complacency, and complacency robs you of the life you are meant to live.

> **Never be satisfied, but always be grateful.**

Your want will require you to think differently. It will require you to be around people who are thinking much bigger. If you want to create massive transformation, understand that want requires us to stretch; stretching is part of the deal. If you're not stretching, you won't do anything with inspiration. Passion makes life inspiring and amazing.

How do you constantly push yourself to the limits? You never do it alone. You surround yourself with great mentors. You build a great inner circle. You absorb great information every day. (I will talk more about mentoring in chapter 13.)

My mentor used to tell me, "You have to do it by yourself, but you can never do it alone."

> **You have to do it by yourself, but you can never do it alone.**

The real questions, again, are these: (1) What do you really want? (2) What price are you going to pay? (3) Are you willing to pay that price? Those are the only three questions you have to answer in order to propel yourself forward.

Key Points in This Chapter

- Clearly define what you really want in life more than anything else. This is the starting point of transformation.
- Consider your hidden commitments—ideas and beliefs that are holding you back from pursuing your true desires.

- Understand the three parts of the mind—the conscious, the subconscious, and the body—and how they work together.
- Discipline your conscious mind to accept and reject ideas.
- Practice the techniques offered above for turning a want into a strong desire, such as repeating affirmations and visualizing the desired outcome.
- Be willing to pay the price required to achieve your goals. This includes activities such as building discipline and working outside your comfort zone.

CHAPTER 3

Your Goal Must Become a Standard

Standard always wins. Over the past twenty years, standard has changed my life—and my clients' lives—significantly. The concept of standard is extremely important. Most people only activate their standards when they get upset enough, but standard, consciously created, will massively transform your life.

One day I was sitting in a hotel in Dallas, where I had a business meeting. The hotel was disgusting. There were cigarette butts everywhere in the meeting rooms. I called my business partner, Mykie Stiller, and said, "I've got to shift hotels." Then my wife, Veronica, said, "We're only going to be in this hotel for another day and a half." She didn't want to move.

At this point, standard had a big impact on my life. I called my brother and asked him to recommend a nicer hotel around Dallas. He found me a hotel about forty minutes away, the Rosewood, and I told my wife, "We're leaving."

When we left, everybody thought I was crazy, perhaps a little too dramatic. But I have changed my life because of standards, and if something bothered me, I would shift it even if it cost me more money.

We checked into the Rosewood, a beautiful resort hotel, and I suggested to Veronica that we go to the lobby bar and have dinner. When we sat down, she said, "Oh, my God, look who's sitting next to us."

She had noticed Jerry Jones, the owner of the Dallas Cowboys. Now I'm an avid sports fan, but I'm a serious Dallas Cowboys fan. She encouraged me to go over and say hello. I said no. She decided to go over. I noticed he had three bodyguards.

"You're man-crushing on him, aren't you?" she said.

Of course, Veronica went over, and he invited us to his table. We spoke for five minutes, and he said, "It's great to meet you," Just small talk.

We went back to our table and finished our meal. As soon as he was about to leave, he walked over to our table and said, "I want to thank you for being a Dallas Cowboys fan." He said he had paid for our dinner.

He spent the next twelve to fifteen minutes talking to us and asked about our kids and our family. But I started picking his brain about entrepreneurship with all his years of building top-end companies in addition to the Dallas Cowboys.

He gave me some of the biggest ideas I've ever received, and it all came back to me. I told Veronica, "Do you see why standard always wins? You're always rewarded by upholding your standards." In this case, moving to a nicer hotel gave us an experience of a lifetime.

When I came home from that trip, I started implementing the high-level ideas he shared with me. Both Veronica and I realized that that would not have happened if we had never left the other hotel. That's why this chapter is so critical to transformation.

I have a client, Joe. For one year, Joe and I just worked on his standards, and it created the greatest impact in his life. He called me and said, "All we've been working on is standards, and it changed my life."

World-class performers are never done growing. They're never starting and stopping. Their personal growth and transformation are sacred. They have a healthy obsession about constantly wanting to learn more and seeing themselves always as a beginner. Every master was always a beginner. I always see myself as a beginner, and I encourage you to do the same.

Your Goal Must Become a Standard

World-class performers are never done growing.

Individuals with high standards are constantly and consistently reinventing themselves. World-class performers believe in themselves, because they keep raising their standards. They know they're capable of more, and they're motivated.

Before we dive deeply into standards, I want you to take a moment to ask yourself what habits no longer work with the life you want to create, and make a list of them. Then ask yourself the second question: what habits must I install to make this year the best year of my life? The answer to this question will set you free.

Of all the judgments we make, none are more important than those we make on ourselves according to our own internal standards. Motivational speaker Denis Waitley observes that personal standards are critical to transformation. Our standards bring our results either up to our new standard or down to what we've always done.

Create a standard that is so high that everything in your environment will move up to it. Most people make the critical mistake of living according to their past instead of bringing their results up to the standard of living they want. They bring themselves down to their current standard.

Our personal standard is our DNA for success. Our happiness is connected to our standards. Look at yourself and at the joy and fulfillment you have. Understand that they are related to your standards.

It is impossible to exceed the standards you set for yourself. Your standards always set your baseline as well as your destination. They are your most important core value. When you put the proper standards in place, you will achieve your goals much more rapidly.

Similarly, your income will never exceed your standards. Raising your standards is the ultimate self-improvement hack for earning more money. Most people think that earning more money requires a new business strategy, better investments, or the perfect opportunity, but the truth is, your financial reality is a direct reflection of what you're willing to accept. If you want to earn more, the law of assumption again comes up.

The first step isn't chasing money: it's raising your standards for what you demand from yourself. Your income always matches your standards, not your potential. Plenty of people are capable of earning six or seven figures, but they don't because their standards allow for procrastination, inconsistency, and low-effort work.

If you expect to be wealthy but tolerate excuses, distractions, or comfort, your bank account will always reflect that. The second you refuse to accept average effort, your results will rise to match your new standard. High standards eliminate low-income habits. People are not broke because they want to be broke. They're broke because they settle for low-value work, distractions, and inconsistent action.

Wealthy people set high standards for their use of time, the value they provide, and the money they will accept earning. Raise your standard for productivity, skill development, and financial discipline, and your income will follow. The marketplace always pays for value, not effort. You don't get paid for working hard. You get paid for the value you bring to the marketplace. If your standard is just, "I'm going to work harder; I'm going to grind harder," you will stay stuck in a low-income cycle. If your standard is to be the best at what you do, your earning potential skyrockets.

Ask yourself daily and journal these questions:
- How can I increase my value?
- How can I solve bigger problems?
- How can I continually serve at a higher level?

Wealth flows to those who expect it. In the earlier chapters, I shared that you always receive what you expect, because your expectation controls your behaviors. People with low financial standards say, "I hope I make more money." But wishing and hoping have no power. People with high standards say, "I will not accept earning less than X amount per month."

> **Three Essential Questions**
>
> 1. How can I increase my value?
> 2. How can I solve bigger problems?
> 3. How can I continually serve at a higher level?

When you raise your income standard, you start making decisions that align with that reality. You make better investments, take on smarter risks, and enjoy higher-paying opportunities.

The market always meets you where your expectations are set. A high standard eliminates low-paying environments. If you allow yourself to stay in underpaid jobs, charge too little for your services, or get involved in toxic business deals or stagnant industries, you'll never break out.

The fastest way to earn more is to stop tolerating situations that keep you stuck.

The fastest way to earn more is to stop tolerating situations that keep you stuck. Surround yourself with people who challenge your financial standards. Invest in knowledge, and position yourself. In high-income environments, you have to become very intentional about the circle you operate in. If you're in a circle that thinks six figures is a lot of money, you'll always have a standard that matches that. If you rise to a circle of people who are creating seven and eight figures, just being in their environment will raise your standard immediately.

Higher earners don't have bigger dreams; they have higher standards. Your financial situation isn't just about opportunity. It's about what you refuse to tolerate. If you want to earn more, stop chasing money and start raising your standards. The moment you decide that your current income is no longer acceptable, you'll take the actions necessary to create wealth.

Wealth never comes from chasing money. It comes from raising your worth. Standards raise your worth right away. Goals are what you want; standards are what you accept. A goal is something you aspire to achieve, but a standard is the level below which you refuse to live. Standards are always my top core value. Goals push you forward, but standards dictate your daily actions. You may make it your goal to get in shape, but if your standard allows for skipping workouts and eating poorly, you'll never get there. You may have an admirable goal of building a successful business, but if your standard tolerates inconsistency and excuses, success will always be out of reach.

The fastest way to earn more is to stop tolerating situations that keep you stuck. When you raise your standards, you automatically elevate your results. You no longer tolerate anything inferior. When you refuse to lower your standards, you force everything around you to rise. Your results will rise, your relationships will rise, your opportunities will rise, and your life will improve enormously.

Mediocrity can't survive in a high-standard environment. People with low standards don't like people with high standards, and people with high standards don't like being around people with low standards. They don't understand each other. When you set the bar and hold the line, you attract people who respect your values, opportunities that match your ambitions, and success that aligns with your discipline.

Everything changes the moment you decide that good enough is no longer good enough.

Everything changes the moment you decide that good enough is no longer good enough. You stop settling, you start growing, and the world begins to respond to the new version of you.

You don't rise to your goal. You always rise to your standards. Refusing to lower your standards isn't about being perfect. It's about being committed to your highest potential. Raising your standards shapes a great identity.

Your Goal Must Become a Standard

Our philosophy creates our standard, and our standard creates our story. Our story in turn creates our identity, and our identity creates our results. Your identity isn't defined by what you say. It's built by what you repeatedly tolerate and demand from yourself. When you raise your standards, you don't merely change what you do, you transform who you are. The moment you decide you won't settle for anything less than excellence, your mindset shifts. You stop seeing yourself as someone who tries. You become someone who *does*.

When you commit to higher standards and follow through, you build self-respect, confidence, and an identity rooted in discipline. Your standards dictate your daily habits, and those habits shape your self-image. People don't admire those who settle. They respect those who demand more from themselves.

As you elevate your standards, you become a person of influence, a leader. Others want to follow your standards. Determine the people you want to be associated with, create opportunities, and experience life. The stronger your identity, the more you will naturally align with excellence. Mediocre situations and people will no longer fit in your life. When high standards become a part of you, you don't back down. Even when things get hard, you become someone who doesn't negotiate with weakness, excuses, or distractions. Your commitment becomes unbreakable.

Your identity is built by your standards. If you want to change your life, don't just set bigger goals. Raise what you demand from yourself every single day.

A great standard to implement—and one that I've implemented for years—is that you are going to beat your personal best from the day before, every day. The moment you do, you don't just change what you achieve, you change who you become. You can change the five top standards:

- Standard of thinking
- Standard of identity
- Standard of attitude
- Standard of action
- Standard of service.

Five Basic Standards

1. Thinking
2. Identity
3. Attitude
4. Action
5. Service

Standard of Thinking

Here are five steps for implementing your thinking framework:
- Set a standard that you're going to refuse to think one thought outside of what you want.
- Refuse to let the outside world control you in any way.
- Refuse to let the world control your attitude, your thinking, or your emotions.
- Accept and reject from your future self, from your goal already achieved.
- Think every thought, every action, every feeling from the state of your goal already achieved.

Standard of Identity

Work with a bigger idea of yourself daily. Consistently focus on working outside your comfort zone by 1 percent or more every day. Make the move before you're ready; that's when magic will start happening for your identity. Do one thing out of your comfort zone, one activity, one hard conversation every day, and your identity will explode.

Standard of Attitude

Look for the good in everything. Train yourself to only look for the good. When you get cut off in traffic, look for the good in it. When you win, look for the good in it. When you have a setback, look for the good too.

Have high expectations for yourself. Remind yourself that you don't receive what you want in life; you receive what you expect, because your expectations control your behavior.

Always come from an attitude of letting go and being detached. This will speed up your goal achievement process.

Standard of Action

Do it now. Do everything urgently, and do it right away. The moment you have resistance, go against the resistance. Enter into the spirit of your task. Everything you do comes from the flow state.

Trust your training. Don't come from your head; come from your heart. Be intentional. Intention is frequency of thought. Always come from the outcome already achieved before you even start.

Standard of Service

Always leave everybody better off than you found them. Give them compliments. Go the extra mile with your service. There are not many people on that extra mile: it is your greatest competitive advantage. Constantly focus on how you can improve your skill set.

Key Points in This Chapter
- Set high personal standards and understand how they can transform your life.
- Standards are crucial for success, as they dictate your daily actions and determine your results. Raising standards is the ultimate self-improvement hack.
- Wealthy people set very high standards for themselves in terms of productivity, skill development, and financial discipline. This approach leads to higher incomes.
- When you raise your standards, you stop tolerating mediocrity and low-paying environments. Instead, you

surround yourself with people and opportunities that match your new standards.
- Standards shape your identity and mindset. Committing to higher standards builds self-respect, confidence, and discipline.
- Consider the five key standards to implement: standard of thinking, standard of identity, standard of attitude, standard of actions, and standard of service.

CHAPTER 4

Programming: The Invisible Script Running Your Life

When I was struggling, I didn't understand how deeply my programming was keeping me stuck in worry, doubt, and fear. Once I started to understand, it changed my results almost immediately.

Success is not a straight line. It is never linear. It's a roller coaster of learning opportunities. It is always up and down. The goal is never the money. The goal is always freedom. Money is just a tool that is going to lead to freedom and fulfillment in doing what you love and loving what you're doing.

The pivotal moment is right now. The point is shifting from what you don't want to fully committing to and pursuing what you absolutely do want. This is how you really want to live.

Time is a tool. Build aggressive deadlines with your goals. What's stopping you from achieving your five-year goal in six to twelve months? You don't need to take years to accomplish the goal in your mind. If you learn how to focus on the right things, it will take ninety days. Quantum leaps are achieved in ninety days when you have the right processes.

A year ago I was working with a client, who called me and told me that he accomplished an enormous goal. He recounted how our conversation started when he decided to be mentored by me. At the time he said, "Arash, it's going to take me five years to achieve this goal."

"Maybe, or maybe you could do it in two years."

"What are you talking about?"

"Every time I set a goal, I set aggressive deadlines, because I want to leverage time. I want you to do that. What if you just accepted that you're going to achieve your five-year goal in two years and we get to work on upgrading your programming, your standards, and your processes? I guarantee you will accomplish it much sooner than in five years."

On this later call, my client said, "Arash, you sold me short. I actually did it in fourteen months," and we both started laughing.

He used time as a tool. What we had to do was upgrade his programming.

Most people let circumstances and outside results dictate their actions. That keeps them operating from the same ideas that are dominating their subconscious mind, and they think the same thoughts in their conscious mind.

Why do people do this? Why do people let the outside dictate when they can achieve a goal, what they can accomplish, and who they are? Why would anyone choose ideas that produce the same results or results they don't want?

This kind of person is not thinking. Their old programming is running them. Our programming is like a computer. If we don't upgrade the software, we're going to keep getting the same results.

From time to time, your smartphone will ask you to upgrade the software. If you don't, the phone will not work properly. The same is true in life. If we want to achieve more, we have to upgrade our software. But let's start with the process of a quantum leap, because there is no reason to upgrade our software unless we want to create something far greater, something that will stretch us to grow further.

The process of a quantum leap is always about elimination. Most people are doing too many things and underperforming. I want you to tattoo this on your brain: *less is more*.

Less is more.

Martial arts master Bruce Lee used to say he was never worried about his opponents who practiced 10,000 moves. He was worried about an opponent who practiced one move 10,000 times.

Similarly, Apple cofounder Steve Jobs said, "People think focus means saying yes to the thing you have to do. But that's not what it means at all. Focus means saying no to the hundreds of other ideas that are great." First, you have to determine: what is that one thing? Then you say no to everything else that is not that one thing.

When I was struggling, I was doing too many tasks. When I created massive success and massive transformation, I committed to doing a few things in a great way. The quantum leap is about eliminating everything that drains your energy: relationships that don't work, everything that no longer serves you, and everything that others can do better than you. To change your programming and transform your life completely, you first have to build a new model, which makes the old model outdated and obsolete. The world rewards conditioning behaviors that are preludes to success.

If you want to look at how you are currently programmed on a subconscious level, you simply have to observe your results in every area of your life.

How do you change your programming? You have to eliminate the behaviors that are sabotaging you. Behaviors create belief, and behaviors are what you're willing to do and not willing to do. To build enormous ideas and change your programming, you have to understand that the idea that is dominating your subconscious mind is reflected in your results.

To change programming, go back to your mind. As we've already seen, you have a conscious mind, a subconscious mind, and a body. We have sensitive antennae that help us see, hear, smell, taste, and touch. Now our programming is no dummy. It always wants to protect us and stay comfortable. It constantly wants us to stay in our comfort zone, and it will channel this desire right to our senses. Our senses in turn will constantly get us to see our current results.

Our intellectual mind has higher faculties that God has given us. These are our superpowers. You change your programming through your memory, your perception, your will, your imagination, your intuition, and your reasoning.

Your memory is amazing, once you understand how to leverage it. I teach my clients to look only at positive memories. I constantly say, "You can think about the birth of your child. Go right back into that emotional state; you'll be in that vibration." That's how you activate memory for your perception.

Your perception is how you see the world. The late inspirational speaker and author Wayne Dyer used to say, "When you change the way you look at things, the things you look at change." That's perception. Our perception creates how we see the world right now. You're not seeing the world as it is. You're seeing it as you are currently programmed.

**You're not seeing the world as it is.
You're seeing it as you are currently programmed.**

Your will is your ability to hold one idea on the screen of your mind without distraction from any other idea. Your will is critical for creating bigger and better results—and for your work habits.

Your imagination is the greatest tool you've been given. It will take you to places you've never even dreamed of. As I've already noted, when you accept an idea, your imagination gives it to your subconscious mind.

Your intuition, your sixth sense, is always talking to you, but are you listening; are you reasoning? Your reasoning is your ability to think. Most people have no idea that they even have these intellectual faculties, but they are your superpowers.

I encourage you to pick one of these faculties and work on it for thirty days. Once you start making it an absolute strength, go to another faculty for thirty days. These are extremely important for changing your results.

Your faculties are in your conscious mind. The way you are currently using them is creating your current program. But when you use your imagination—visualizing and accepting and rejecting ideas throughout the day and getting emotionally involved only in what you want—you are embedding a new program inside of you. Once you change the program, the results have to change.

Changing programming demands explosive thinking. It demands emotional involvement and a sense of urgency. Since you can never get results beyond your current level of thinking, you have to leverage your results and look at them: they will tell you where you need to upgrade your thinking. Are you letting the past or your current results dictate how you think? Or are you letting your future self, the desired state of how you want to live, dictate how you think?

The only difference between those who have failed and those who have succeeded is in their habits. Thinking is a habit. I challenge you to become relentless about thinking abundantly in everything you do. Create a new program, which first starts with knowing what you want and then deciding that you are going to commit all in:

I will do whatever it takes because my goal will demand whatever it takes. It always takes whatever it takes.

The next step is to *take extreme ownership*. You are absolutely responsible for all the results you're currently getting. Take responsibility; understand you're the only problem you're ever going to have and you're the only solution you're ever going to have. When you do, you will take back your power to transform your life instead of being a victim to circumstances and letting the outside dictate your results.

If you look at great leaders, they always take responsibility for whatever problem that's going on in the organization. You'll know a great leader because they always are the first to say, "This was my fault," even if it wasn't. That's understanding the responsibility of a leader. When you take responsibility, you significantly increase your self-esteem.

There's never been an easier time to create great freedom, wealth, and transformation than there is right now, because there's never been a time where so many victims have been blaming so many outside circumstances. Your competitive advantage is your mind and your imagination. They are critical for complete transformation and complete freedom.

> Your competitive advantage is your
> mind and your imagination.

The industrialist Andrew Carnegie told Napoleon Hill, author of *Think and Grow Rich*, that any idea held in the mind and emphasized, whether it is feared or revered, will begin at once to clothe itself in the most convenient and appropriate physical form available.

Your thinking is critical. If you are thinking only about what you want and reject everything that is not what you want, the repetition of this abundant thinking will change your programming. Changing your programming will alter your vibration, and you will in turn change your actions. You will know that you have changed your programming because the types of thoughts you have are different, the types of actions you take are different, and your results will change by law.

This point comes back to the question I keep asking. Transformation demands that you know this answer: what do you really want more than anything else in the world?

Once again, if you do not have a want and you have not created a magnificent obsession, there is no reason to change your programming. We never justify our wants; we own them. We radically accept our wants. When you radically accept them, you're starting to work on transformation.

Transformation never occurs when the result happens. Transformation occurs when you decide to kill off your old emotional state, stop being obsessed with what's wrong, and start creating the life you really want. If you don't know what you want, you're always going to drift. You're always going to start or stop.

My mentor had me study Thomas Troward very closely. Troward was a New Thought leader in the 1800s who wrote an insightful essay called "Principle over Precedent." It is essential to master this essay in order to create a completely new program and a new life.

It's always a matter of thinking about what you want instead of present results and circumstances. Most people make the cause the effect and the effect the cause. They think the cause is not having enough money. But money is always the effect, not the cause. The cause is always us. It's our thinking. It's our programming.

If you allow present results to control your thinking, you will continue to create from the same program and will constantly produce the same results. It's called the *fulfilling cycle of doom*—thinking the same thoughts, feeling the same feelings, taking the same actions, while expecting different results. A definition of insanity, often attributed to Albert Einstein, is doing the same thing over and over but expecting different results.

Make a firm commitment to yourself that from this moment on, you absolutely refuse to let your present results influence you in any way. Why would you want to do that? The present results are created from your past self, not from who you currently are.

Programming Shift

To create a massive programming shift, you must:

1. Know where you are.
2. Know where you are going.

You must know two things to create a massive programming shift: you have to know where you are and where you're going. That doesn't seem too difficult; it is so simple and obvious. Why, then, are so many people stuck? If all you had to know was where you are and where you're going, you would have to fill in the gap between those two, and it is always your decisions, your thinking, your disciplines, and your actions. Stephen R. Covey, author of *The Seven Habits of*

Highly Effective People, wrote, "Between stimulus and response there is a space. In that space is our power to choose our response. In our response lies our growth and our freedom."

Do you know where you want to go? My guess is that since you're reading this book, you do you want something greater. Most people know where they want to go. Then why are they still getting the same results? Because even though they may have a great goal, they're constantly living their lives from their present circumstances only. Why are they doing that? Because the program is running them. The program is deeply embedded.

To create a new program, you have to be intentional about thinking, feeling, and acting in accordance with what your goal demands. Changing a program requires space, repetition, and emotional impact. In the last case, the impact often comes from something negative: a catastrophe, a divorce, a sudden loss in the family.

The best way to change a program is repetition. As I've already mentioned, I advise my clients to create audio recordings of their goal already achieved. Say this (or tailor it to your goal): *I'm so happy and grateful now that I'm in the very best shape of my life. I'm filled with energy. Every cell of my being is completely healthy,* I ask them to record that and listen to it over and over again.

Think about how we created our programs in the first place. Since the age of five, we have been listening to other people. At that point, everything in our environment was creating our program, and it was based on other people—parents, grandparents, peers.

Today you want to consciously create your program. You don't want anybody creating your program but you, so you have to master the art of accepting and rejecting ideas from your goal. Practice autosuggestion. Practice mental rehearsal by visualizing and listen to the recording of what you want. Listen to it when you're driving. The more you listen to it, the faster your program will change. Repetition is the mother of all learning, and it will be your silent partner in changing your program.

Repetition is the mother of all learning.

Again, I want you to look at where you are right now and think about what you really want the most. *What is my goal?* Understand that there is always a brick wall between where you are and where you want to go. That's your programming.

How do you knock down that brick wall? You make an all-in, irrevocable, committed decision. You tell yourself that this is what you're going to achieve, regardless of how long it takes. You commit to the right processes. You listen to your recording. You act like the person who has already achieved that goal. You make every decision from the perspective of that person, and you become relentless about thinking abundantly.

When you make that definite decision, you knock down that wall. Now you have an open space to go from where you are to where you want to go. Understand that you achieve your chosen goal by changing your program. You cannot continue operating with the same program.

Paradigms and programming can blind our views and limit our perspective. As I said earlier, you're not seeing the world as it is: you're seeing it as you're currently programmed. This is a black-and-white deal. It does not matter how hard you work, how nice of a person you are, or how many hours you put in: if the program docs not change, the results will remain the same from one year to the next. When programs stay in control, nothing changes.

Correcting limiting thoughts is not about being perfect, but it is a matter of consistency. You have to constantly direct your mind back towards the person you want to be. Like driving a car, it's about constant correction. When you start to veer, you have to straighten the car. The same is true of the mind. You're constantly turning yourself in the direction of your goal.

You may be saying, "Arash, I am really working on only thinking about what I want, but for the last several months, nothing has changed."

Why has nothing changed? Why do people achieve some goals but not others? It's because of this one key: *hidden commitment*. People often operate with hidden commitment that send out a double-binding message. They want to be successful, yet the rest of the day, they see themselves as they are presently. They're affirming, *I am successful. I'm living a life of freedom*, yet all day long they're focusing on problems. They're focusing only on what's missing.

In other words, they are coming from doubt, which creates worry, which creates fear, and that is a double-binding message: it is the opposite of what they want. They want to increase their business ten times over, but they are always thinking about what's wrong. The aware person realizes that this is the very definition of insanity.

Be done with that. Discipline your thinking. Upgrade your programming. Listen to your recordings; practice autosuggestion every three hours. Visualize ten minutes a day. Make every decision as the person who's already achieved that goal. That person now is transforming into and aligning with a new identity. It's called *praxis*, defined as *customary practice or activity*.

Aligning your beliefs, behaviors, and actions with your desire will change your results. No longer will you be creating a double-binding message; you'll be creating breakthrough after breakthrough—and not just little breakthroughs. When you align yourself only with your desired state—where you're thinking what you would think and feel and taking actions that you would take in that state—you create massive results.

We want to eliminate conflicting, double-binding messages. Napoleon Hill had a great quote in *Think and Grow Rich*. He said there's a difference between wishing for a thing and being ready to receive it. No one is ready for a thing until he believes he can acquire it. The state of mind must be belief, not mere hope or wish. Open-mindedness is essential for belief.

There's a difference between wishing for a thing and being ready to receive it.

I always ask my clients, "Are you ready to receive?" They say yes. Then I say, "Well, are you operating? Are you operating consistently out of your comfort zone?"

"No."

"Are you doing the recordings?"

"No."

"Are you taking bold action?"

"No."

"You're just wishing and hoping, but you're not ready to receive."

In my twenty years of studying this philosophy every day, I've discovered that the universe will never give us anything until we're ready to keep it. So we have to be willing to take the necessary steps before we're programmed to take them. That's how massive paradigm shifts happen.

Let me ask you a question: are you willing to fail at your future self, than succeed at your present self? Because that is essential for creating the new program.

Once you change the program and understand desire, you know it's a done deal. Desire and expectation, mixed together, are the most important attitudes for creating attractive forces. Desire without expectation is idle wishing or hoping. It's useless. Most people try to achieve a goal by willing themselves to achieve it. In the beginning, you will yourself to develop the habits, create the feelings, and take the actions necessary, but without a shift in your programming, you're going to drift.

Many people desire great things but never achieve them because they lack expectation. Desire takes you to the five-yard line; expectation scores the touchdown. When you constantly expect what you persistently desire, your ability to attract becomes effortless.

Have you ever wondered why some people turn whatever they touch to gold, while others are trying hard but still struggle? Because success is automatically based on programming. Failure is automatic. It is time to create your automatic success mechanism by focusing on executing the right processes. What are those right processes? Making every decision from your goal already achieved. It's not good enough just to visualize and then go back to your old self for the rest of the day. You must think abundantly regardless of the appearances.

Put an alarm on your phone and set it for three hours. When it rings, repeat your goal. Visualize it for ten minutes a day. That is how to change your programming.

In a recent podcast, a top movie producer said that as soon as he wakes up, he mentally rehearses for sixty minutes. To the brain, mental rehearsal is real. It is as if what it is seeing is happening right now. Top performers in every industry rehearse mentally. I don't think you have to do it for sixty minutes, but I definitely think you should make it a practice for ten minutes. Discipline your senses to see what you would see if you had you already achieved the goal.

Desire always creates the positive force of attraction. When an individual relentlessly desires something, it's a magnificent obsession. They set up a force that connects them with the invisible force of the good they desire. If that desire weakens or changes, that force is disconnected.

Your program wasn't created overnight, and it's not going to change overnight. Most people stop doing the tedious programming work because they don't see immediate results, and their goal and their desire drift away. But if you remain constant in practicing the processes, the frameworks, and the connections with your desire, the good will be realized every single time.

Understand that the program is designed to defend the current system. It is like a con man, always trying to trick you: "Why do you want more? You're doing better than most." But every time you rationalize, you're lying to yourself. The program is running your life. It is always in solid support of *not* getting the results you want. It will confuse you, it will convince you, and it will get you back to doing what you used to do. Instead, you want your desire, your goal, and your future self to run your life.

Programming

*You want your desire, your goal,
and your future self to run your life.*

Whatever we plant in our subconscious mind and nourish with repetition and emotion will one day become reality. Most people's emotions are stronger than their mindset. That's why they're letting the outside control them. Train yourself so that your mindset is stronger than your emotions. Training your mindset by repeating the frameworks and processes I'm giving here, you will create transformation and quantum leaps in ninety days.

Key Points in This Chapter

- Subconscious programming deeply affects your life and your results. It's important to upgrade your programming and thought patterns to achieve greater success and freedom.
- Success is not linear, but a roller coaster of learning opportunities. The goal should be freedom, not just money.
- Quantum leaps in goal achievement are possible through eliminating distractions, focusing on a few key priorities, and upgrading your programming.
- To change programming, you must use your intellectual faculties, like memory, perception, will, imagination, intuition, and reasoning.
- Repetition and emotionally connecting with your desired vision and goal are critical for reprogramming the subconscious mind.
- It is essential to make a firm, all-in commitment to your goal and to make decisions from the mindset of the person who has already achieved that goal.

CHAPTER 5

Your Results Reflect Your Identity

Before I was ready to step into my seven-figure self-image, I decided firmly that I was done protecting myself and playing it safe. I can recall the first few calls I had with Bob Proctor. He said, "Arash, for anyone to create significant results, they have to have a significant identity."

I made a firm decision to take decisive action before I was ready. I stopped letting the outside dictate what was comfortable or what I was willing to do and not do. I chose clarity over complexity. I stopped overthinking and started thinking like the seven-figure version of myself.

What was that seven-figure version? I had no idea. I was just studying other people who were creating a seven-figure income. I studied how they talked, how they walked, how they executed ideas in these moments. Before I knew it, I was making an identity shift. I was becoming the person who started creating success automatically. I started becoming process-driven in my execution. I aligned my daily actions with my new self-image, and I started building unstoppable momentum. I focused on standards over emotions. I led with who I decided I was, not with the person I was then based on current results.

This wasn't just a breakthrough: it was a transformation that happened in weeks. Creating success is always a tug-of-war between the old you and the new you, between your fears and your dreams. If your fears win, you lose.

Freedom requires peeling away fear and attachment. What I would like you to ask yourself these questions. Write your responses in your journal:
- What are my greatest attachments right now?
- Am I attached to the past?
- Am I attached to what other people are thinking?
- Am I attached to the *how*?
- What is my fear showing me?
- Am I suppressing the fear?
- Is fear my greatest hidden commitment?

The answers to these questions will free you up and unleash the best version of you. You want to understand. As Wallace D. Wattles, author of the classic *Science of Getting Rich*, wrote, "The universe desires you to have everything you want to have."

The universe desires you to have everything you want to have.

Let's accept that idea. The universe is a friendly universe once we start working in harmony with its laws.

You have to decide to upgrade your identity, and, again, it can't just be any type of decision. It has to be an irrevocable, committed decision built by following through with habits and deciding to be that person every day.

Self-image is an inside game. It is the most honest picture of how we really see ourselves. Your self-image is the foundation of your success, and it is always creating your results. When you change the image on the inside, you'll be rewarded by the change on the outside. Everything begins with changing the concept of yourself. I encourage you to make it a declaration and a habit that you are going to commit to seeing yourself as much bigger than you currently see yourself.

The concept of "be, do, have" is powerful. Commit to *being* more than you've ever been, which will cause you to *do* more than you've ever done. And I promise you, you're going to *have* more than you could have ever dreamed of. Be. Do. Have.

Be honest with yourself. When you are not, you destroy your possibilities for growth, because you're suppressing everything inside of you. I used to resist self-image work because I thought that was bringing out my weaknesses. But I discovered that every time a weakness came up, it became a strength for me, and I created a healthy relationship with my self-image.

Let's discover your self-image regarding different aspects of your life. Answer the following questions in detail. Your responses will show you the dominant image in your mind regarding these different topics.

- What do I really believe about wealth?
- What do I believe about my business or the ability to build a business?
- What do I believe about my health?
- What do I believe about my own worthiness to prosper?
- Do I believe that I deserve to prosper?

Now we are going to build a new model of a much greater version of you—your future self. To do this, you want to be willing to give yourself permission to soar, to have the courage to bet on yourself.

Self-image is all about you. It's all understanding who you are. Understand that you are infinite. There's no end to where you could take yourself. Your spiritual DNA is absolutely perfect. It requires no modification or improvement. It is all-knowing. It is all-powerful. It is ever present and it is the real you. You have access to all the knowledge in the world. Knowledge is easy to acquire now that you have access to all the power in the world.

You'll see stories on the news that say a hundred-pound woman lifted up a car because her baby was underneath. She was using all the power. You have access to all the power too. It could be with you when you're traveling on any continent, because it is the real you.

Are you truly what and who you pretend to be? That's an interesting question. If you're not really making it happen, it's because you are coming from the physical side of you and you're not understanding who you are.

Realize that your job is to become more and more aware of the infiniteness inside of you and that your spiritual DNA is perfect. There is nothing you need to fix for yourself. You want to build the greatest version of you.

It all starts with building a bigger idea of yourself. I want you to build an enormous idea of yourself. I want you to create a paragraph-long declaration of the person you want to become. For example: *I'm so happy and grateful now that I am living my dreams and I'm living a life of freedom, doing what I love and loving what I'm doing. I am confident, I am disciplined. I act on ideas right away, and I am living a world-class life.*

Then you want to come from that image in everything you do. Another version inside of you is dying to come out even while you're reading these pages. Is there fire burning in you, or are you wondering if this is real? Understand that there's another version of you who can do ten times better than you're currently doing. Your job is to let that person out. How? By deciding who you're going to become.

There's another version of you who can do ten times better than you're currently doing.

You're letting that person out, but identity starts with how you see yourself. Act as if you're the best and nobody is better than you. Adopt the mindset and habits of someone who is on top of their game. Exude excellence. Set a standard so high that your results elevate automatically. This is not arrogance; it's certainty. It's carrying yourself with certainty in everything you do.

This takes me back to a conversation that developed this philosophy for me. I was having a phone call with Bob Proctor, and he said,

"Arash, let me ask you a question. Do you see yourself as the best in the world at what you do?"

This was six months into our relationship, and I said, "No, but I think I'm becoming one of the best."

"From this moment on, I want you to see yourself as the best," he said. "I want you to see yourself as better than I am."

"Bob, how am I going to do that? You have all these years of experience."

"Forget about the years of experience. Do you know why I am so good at what I do?"

"Why?"

"Because I'm never worried about what anybody else is doing. I see myself as the best, and I want you to see yourself as the best."

Years later, Bob and I were sitting in a coffee shop before an event that he was hosting.

I told him, "You unleashed me the day you gave me permission to see myself as the best in the world."

"I remember the conversation very well," he said. "Arash, a lot of people are not soaring because they're seeing themselves too small. I wanted to see you."

Once I started seeing myself as the best, I walked into the best version of me. When you act as if you're the best, magic happens, and you start believing it. Your story about you changes, and when you believe it, you become it.

Right now you may be reading these words and thinking, "I am not close to being the best. I'm really facing a lot of adversity. My results are terrible." What if I told you, who cares? The beauty of this principle is, it works even if you're not the best right now. I see you as unlimited potential.

Many people hear a voice in their head that says, "I'm not good enough." That voice is a liar. Don't listen to it. It is based on your ego and the past. Acting as if you're the best doesn't mean ignoring your weaknesses. It creates an image of who your future self is going to be.

Let's get into future-self philosophy. There are three parts of ourselves: our present self, our past self, and our future self. Our past

> ### Three Parts of the Self
> 1. The past self
> 2. The present self
> 3. The future self

always comes from the old version of us. Your past self always comes from your old paradigm, your old programming and bondage. Kill off your old self. Your future self is committed to a big goal. That's where freedom is now. Everything always starts from this present moment, from your present self.

We're choosing either our past or our future in everything we do. When you're choosing your past, you default to your past self and you're always thinking, "If I just work harder, I'll get there." You want the person who is coming from their past self to always create better results. Without changing, this will never happen. And your past self is always negotiating with your present self about the future. It's saying, "You're doing better than most. Just keep doing what you're doing." It is a liar. You are meant to soar.

Your past self doesn't have any fuel for inspiration. It has no juice; it has no fire. And if there is no fire, there is no transformation. Your future self is the you that knows how to do things that you could only imagine doing right now. It's the you that wants you to experience life in the grandest way.

When you're coming from your future self, you have a big, ten-times goal, a goal that is worthy of you. You start at the future, and with every decision, you bring it into the present. Every action is driven by the future. You start with the future, your goal, as the lead in everything you do. You free yourself from the past because your past self cannot relate to your future self. Your future self is completely different. Success comes from being in harmony and aligned with your future self. Being separate from your future self will lead to delusion.

Now you have to create a relationship with your future self. This relationship has to be cultivated, just as you cultivate relationships with your friends, colleagues, and children.

I will give you an exercise I give all my elite clients. I would like you to write a letter from your future self congratulating you on what you've accomplished over the last year, as if it is already done.

I use ChatGPT. Open the program and use this prompt: "Write my future self a letter." If you list the characteristics and goals you want, artificial intelligence will write out an emotionally powerful letter. Then read it aloud and record it. (Get into the habit of listening to recordings over and over.) You could write:

Future self, I am so happy that I decided to tap into your wisdom. In everything I do, I come from you. You are giving me more and more information of how I become you. Over the last twelve months, I've absolutely transformed my life. I have never been more courageous. I've never had more guts. I have eliminated all the things that I needed to quit. I have achieved my goal of X.

Listen to this letter over and over again. You're going to create a connection with your future self, and you're going to transform your identity.

Everything you do for yourself is an investment in your future self. Your future drives what you do in the present. The future also decides which parts of the past will come along with you, such as valuable experiences and achievements. The future decides the parts of the past that you will bring to that future. We are always choosing the future with our imagination: something bigger, bolder, and better.

Changing your identity is about becoming 1 percent better every day. Think about the ideal image that you want to create for yourself, and then define the area that you're going to focus on for the thirty days. For example, *for one month, I'm going to get 1 percent better at acting on ideas. I'm releasing procrastination.* Or it could be, *I'm going to do it now 1 percent better every single day.*

Many people will tell me they've gotten 1 percent better. Then I ask them how they measure it, and they're silent. I offer this: "I will tell you, the best way to leverage 1 percent is to define every thirty days the exact characteristics of your new image. Focus on that characteristic and become 1 percent better every day."

Identity shifts and transformations start and end with falling in love with the best version of yourself that you want to become. When you fall in love with *you*, your life becomes more and more magical.

Going to this new version of you requires completely new habits. It requires letting go of the habits that no longer serve you from the old you. We'll get into that in the next chapter.

Key Points in This Chapter

- Your self-image and identity are the foundation of your success. To achieve significant results, you need to have a significant identity.
- Make an irrevocable decision to upgrade your identity. Commit to becoming the best version of yourself through your daily habits and actions.
- Your past self and fears hold you back, while your future self represents your unlimited potential. Cultivate a relationship with your future self and let it guide your present actions.
- Becoming 1 percent better every day in specific areas related to your ideal self-image is key to transforming your identity.
- Falling in love with the best version of yourself makes your life more magical.

CHAPTER 6

Identity Is a Daily Decision

I started mentoring Stephanie two years ago. Since then, her identity has taken a massive transformation, because she is making daily decisions using the same framework that I'm giving you in this book. She has become a powerhouse in her industry. Stephanie shared with me how shifting her identity has changed her life and how much identity has changed her confidence.

You are no different from Stephanie. That's exactly what's going to happen to you. Identity shifts quickly when we become intentional with our decisions and start coming from our future self. The process of growth from who and what you are to who you want to become is called *the work*. This work is done daily.

You'll always be rewarded by doing the work. Once again, it comes down to the idea that you have to radically accept and see yourself as the person you want to become. You want to make that healthy relationship get better. Your magnificent obsession is about what you get to become, whom you get to fall in love with, and how you can grow.

Let's go back and understand where you are right now versus where you want to be. There is always a gap, and that gap is always going to be your identity. Once you start becoming *more* every day by beating your personal best—by thinking, feeling, acting, and making decisions as the person who's already achieved what you want to achieve—your image and your identity will soar. But it can only happen if you make daily decisions.

Decisions shape our lives. They're creating enormous abundance, enormous impact, and enormous fulfillment, or else we are constantly making decisions from our old self.

We have to release the obsession with being our old self. That is a decision. That's why this chapter is so important, because your subconscious mind will only give you what you feel you deeply deserve.

On a deep, subconscious level, I want you to put your goal in your mind. What is your relationship with this goal? Are you thinking it will be hard to get? I want you to accept the idea that your goal is already done. The only thing you have to do to fill in the gap is to decide to keep growing your image—to fill that identity gap.

What is that identity gap for you? Is it procrastination? Then fix that identity gap to an identity of doing it now. Is it planning to plan before you're ready, or making the move before you're ready? The greatest way to change an image is to start behaving in your new way before you're ready. In so doing, you will create a visceral experience, and you'll become that person instantaneously.

This moment is your time to take liftoff.

We have to ask ourselves these key questions: Is my old story still controlling me? Am I holding back? Am I letting my past define me? Am I letting my past mistakes define me? Have you ever thought that you should be further along than you are right now? Are other people further along than you? Let that go. You're exactly where you should be, but this moment is your time to make liftoff.

Understand that you can skip levels by working and transforming your self-image.

Let's go back to these questions: *What is my hidden commitment right now? My goal is X. What is the person who is achieving that goal doing that I'm not doing? What are their behaviors? When they walk into a room, does their energy influence those present before they even speak?*

There is always that hidden commitment—something in our lives that we think we don't have to deal with, that we think we can bring with us into the future. But I promise you, you will never be able to do that. You have to decide that you're done with protecting yourself from who you want to be. Go all in.

What is it costing you to protect yourself? It is costing you amazing experiences. It's costing you transformation after transformation. It's costing you opportunities, and it's costing you freedom. You, once again, are an amazing story. I'm going to keep repeating that to you over and over, because there's nothing you have to fix. You just have to build *you* and grow *you* and let go of the viral codes that are lying to you.

Your past is just a story, but your story determines your potential. It is your identity. Bulletproof your story and align it with your future self. Writing and recording a letter to your future self (as mentioned in the previous chapter) and repeatedly listening to it over and over will change your story.

What story do you want more than anything else for your future? How you narrate your story affects your present and future behaviors. Always follow your story. If you don't have great behaviors right now, understand that your story is causing them.

Who is the person you want to become? Answer this question without any influence from your past or present. The more clearly you define the characteristics you want for your future self, the easier it will be to become anything you wish. Think about a person who decides they are going to get in the best shape of their life. They start measuring their nutrition, their workouts, and their walks, and all of a sudden they create effortless success.

Consider a person in another camp. They say they are going to eat better, but they never measure what they eat. They sabotage themselves by eating a lot more and working out a lot less than they think. That's identity.

In order to become what you want, you must overcome the old you. In the beginning, the side effect is discomfort. Discomfort is a great sign. Don't resist it. Keep going. Keep persisting. Discomfort is your subconscious mind telling you you're on the right track. Fear is not designed to stop us; it's designed to help us. Most people have a bad relationship with fear. Every time you have a fearful thought, say, "That's good," and keep going.

Discomfort is your subconscious mind telling you you're on the right track.

As the philosopher Ralph Waldo Emerson said, "Do the thing, and you shall have the power." He didn't say, "Imagine the thing." Your identity shifts as a result of what you either do or don't do. You're always choosing your old life or your future world-class life. You're either choosing your old self or your future self. Which are you going to choose? I'm going to give you the future self framework and explain how to implement it.

The Future Self Framework

This is a game changer for achieving transformation, world-class goals, and a life of freedom. The future self framework works like this: everything you do is based on the acceptance of the idea that your goal is achieved.

Every morning, set an intention just for today: You're going to make every decision from the person who's already achieved your goal. You're going to operate with the attitude that you are prosperous, you look only for the good in everything, and you are living the standards of the person who's already achieved your goal.

What are those standards? You act on ideas. You are detached. You are focused only on getting better. All day long, you think, feel, and act like the person who's already achieved your goal. You focus on the few critical disciplines practiced by the person who's already achieved your goal.

What are those disciplines? You focus on the most important activities every day: your highest income-producing activities. In the evening, as soon as you're done with work, observe yourself. Say, "I'm going to observe my day. What were the decisions that I made today? Were they in line with the person who has achieved my goal? What type of attitude did I show? Was it aligned with the person who achieved my goal? Did I live the standards today? Did I think, feel, and act like that person today? Did I implement the disciplines that I committed to in the morning?"

Do this self-assessment without any judgment. Let's say you go four for five; let's say you dropped on your attitude. You don't shame yourself. You say, "I'm going to make sure to double up on my attitude tomorrow."

This future self framework is a game changer. I have a phenomenal client, Mary. Two years ago, I was doing a coaching call with her while I was vacationing in San Diego, and she said, "Arash, I don't know what to do. I'm stuck." I gave her this future self framework.

Our call was short. She said, "That's all I need."

She implemented the future self framework for two months, and she had a windfall. She lives by this framework. Implement it, execute it, and watch it work magic in your life.

If you want to really understand the person you're becoming every day, I will show you how. Set an alarm on your phone at one o'clock in the afternoon and once again at five o'clock in the evening. When the alarm at one goes off, observe the first half of your day and ask yourself what thoughts you were having, what feelings were showing up, and what actions you took. Observing the first part of your day provides the most honest assessment of the person you're becoming. Let's say you crush it; just keep going. But let's say that you've been thinking from the past. For the next half of the day, tell yourself that you are going to be superintentional. Decide to think exactly like the person who's already achieved your goal.

You say, "I'm going to feel pride, I'm going to feel excited, I'm going to feel inspired, and then I'm going to take the most important actions for the rest of the day."

Do that, and you will become your new identity.

I want you to think of the image of the person you want to become. I want you to train yourself to see yourself in your conscious mind the way you want to be. Then I want you to train yourself to feel that you are already that person. This will alter your vibration. When you repeatedly impress, see, and feel yourself as that new person, your body will alter its vibration, and your results will change, but this change will not happen instantaneously. A period of time must lapse before you see it physically.

If you decide to change, your world is going to change. If you change your thinking on both conscious and subconscious levels, you can change the outcomes you experience. It's done through a deliberate and consistent practice of decision.

Let me share with you the most important identity-based behaviors for create a seven-figure identity. Number one is your attitude toward yourself. You want to see yourself as prosperous. You want to see only that you can do it, and you're going to build your courage up.

Identity-based behavior makes your goal definite. Every day, you decide that every day is day one and you're only making decisions from the person who's already achieved the goal. You will leave everyone better off than you found them, and you'll bulletproof your focus.

Distraction is the enemy of identity transformation. You're going to focus on the most important attributes and create the mental equivalent of the person you want to become. You're going to develop an amazing relationship with money. You're going to understand that money is not good or bad, it just is, and you will put all your focus on service. You will act on ideas right away. Acting on ideas will change your identity overnight, because it creates a visceral experience. Commit to willingness to fail at creating your future self, then succeed as your present self. Say this: "I'm willing to fail, fail, fail, and keep pivoting forward, even if I don't see the results, because that is identity transformation in action."

Do everything in a calm, detached, confident manner. Act right away and be willing to face your insecurities, because now you know that your insecurities create your greatest gifts.

Do everything in a calm, detached, confident manner.

Bulletproof your self-talk. Remember what David Schwartz said in his book *The Magic of Thinking Big*: we're speaking either our castles or our funerals into existence. Focus only on the good that you desire. Use your higher faculties and activate your superpowers: your perception, your memory, your reasoning, your imagination, and your intuition. These identity-based behaviors will create a seven-figure self-image for you.

Becoming the best version of yourself isn't a one-time act. It requires you to continually edit your beliefs and upgrade your image. Behaviors that are incongruent with the self won't last. That's why you want to build your behaviors in your imagination: build your thinking pattern, build your emotional state, because that's how you'll engage in lasting behaviors. Strong behaviors lead to strong actions, which in turn develop an impeccable self-image. A permanent paradigm shift is an identity shift. Improvements are only temporary until they become a part of who you are.

I would love your self-talk to be: *I'm the type of person who creates great service. I'm the type of person who makes healthy choices. I'm the type of person who makes quantum leaps a part of my birthright. I'm the type of person who is worthy and deserving of the good that I desire.*

When you show up as the best version of yourself, you are allowing the laws of the universe to work in your favor.

Key Points in This Chapter

- Daily decisions shape our self-image.
- Identity is a daily decision. Acting boldly helps build identity.
- There is always a gap between your current and your desired identities. Closing this gap requires daily intentional decisions and behaviors.
- The future self framework involves setting daily intentions; thinking, feeling, and acting like the person who has already achieved your goals; and reflecting on your progress.
- Practice identity-building behaviors such as cultivating a prosperous attitude, having a clear and definite goal, focusing on high-impact activities, and developing a positive relationship with money and self-talk.
- Identity transformation is a gradual process. It requires persistence, facing discomfort, and a willingness to fail at your future self in order to succeed.

CHAPTER 7

The Goal Achievement Process

The greatest crisis in most people's lives doesn't result from a lack of talent, resources, or opportunity. It's from a lack of powerful stretching and a soul-stirring goal.

Small goals produce small energy, and without fuel, there's no fire. No matter how hard you work, you'll never rise above the target you've set for yourself. I'm going to show you why ordinary goals keep extraordinary success out of reach, and how to set goals that force you to grow, think bigger, and claim the life that's waiting for you.

Imagine getting in your car and driving aimlessly while hoping to end up at a beautiful destination. That's how most people live their lives: without clear, focused, intentional goals. Goals are not optional. They are the GPS of your life. Without them, you drift. You must direct your life with purpose, precision, and power.

This chapter will show you how to set goals that don't just motivate you but move you. Goals are never really about the goal: they're about the version of you that must emerge to achieve them. Challenging goals force you to grow, evolve, and become.

Goal setting is an intellectual exercise toward goal achievement. We'll dive deep into goal setting, because real success isn't about crossing a finish line. It's about transforming into the kind of person who wins in every area of life.

I have a great client, Michael. I had been mentoring him for several months, and one day he got on a call with me. He said, "Arash, I'm just checking the box. I really want to create a massive quantum leap."

I shared with Michael that he had to set ninety-day, big-stretch goals that would really show him what he's capable of. I told him this was going to be the easiest ninety days, because I was going to eliminate most of the things he was doing that were producing so-so results. He agreed.

I made it simple. I crafted four action steps for Michael every day, and I told him goal achievement is about elimination—getting rid of the 80 percent that is not moving the needle.

Michael not only committed to taking those four action steps every day over those first ninety days, but he created the best quarter of his life, and now he's done it three quarters in a row.

Goal achievement happens by exact law. In this chapter, I want to talk about how to achieve world-class goals. World-class goals are where the world-class energy is. There's a lot of fire inside of you, but to achieve a quantum leap like Michael's in ninety days, you have to understand some ground rules:

1. You must be hyperfocused and hyperintentional.
2. You must focus daily on understanding what you're doing that is causing you to grow and what is causing you to be distracted.
3. You must constantly focus on increasing your value and your mission.
4. You must recollect why you want to achieve the goal. When the *why* is big enough, the *how* always takes care of itself.

I want you to think about which goal you would like to achieve more than anything else. Radically accept the idea that it would be impossible for you to fail.

Goal achievement is an art. It's a manipulation of energy from one frequency to another. You jump frequency when you make every decision as the person who's already achieved the goal and have radically accepted that your goal is accomplished. Divorce yourself from the outcome, and never worry about how it's going to happen. Focus only on who you have to become. What can you leverage, and what are your highest-producing activities from the goal?

When you've radically accepted an idea, you'll know, because your goal has become a magnificent obsession. It is always on your mind. Think about the first time you fell in love. That person was always on your mind. Turn your goal into a love story. Your goal has to always be on your mind: it's an obsession; you don't have to try to think about it. It is always consuming you, from the moment you wake up in the morning to the moment you go to sleep.

Make your goal so big that you believe it is impossible. Stretch goals are important. Life is about stretching. When you make a goal so big that in the beginning you believe it's impossible and you start playing with ideas, you make the impossible possible. Every time you make the impossible possible, you're activating your imagination.

Let me give you an example. Let's say that you're earning $100,000 a year, and you want to earn $100,000 a month. Now let's start opening up your imagination. Think, "If I was charging $10,000 per client, all I would need to do was attract ten clients a month." Well, now your mind will start thinking of not only how you can but *why* you can. We want to start by making the goal impossible, and we want to start playing with the ideas.

Suppose you said, "I don't want to work with ten people a month; I want to work with five people a month." Then we say, "How can I increase my product, my idea, or service to so a high value that I could charge $20,000 for it? I would just need to attract five clients a month."

Now you're thinking from the goal. When you are working to the goal, one-timing your results, then doubling, even tripling, your results, you will have a certain number of different strategies from your current ones. But working with world-class energy and a goal that is proportionately huge will cause you to think much bigger. Only a limited number of strategies will work. Every time you get an idea, you'll be able to filter it out and ask, "Is this is from my old self or from the big goal, where the world-class energy is?"

Creating a quantum leap in your goal achievement process requires completely new habits. It requires you to let go of 80 percent of your old life.

I want you to think about your goal right now. I want you to write it down; then create an elimination list. What habits are not in harmony with the world-class goal that you want to achieve? You must eliminate these habits.

What habits are not in harmony with the world-class goal that you want to achieve?

Then make another list. What are the top three habits that you must install, coming from the goal, that will allow you to achieve your world-class goal? What is your stretch goal?

People set three types of goals. There's the average goal. That's a goal somebody's already achieved: it causes no stretch. They've already done it; they're always succeeding from their current self, so there's no growth. Then there's another type of goal: one they've never accomplished, but it's a little bit better than they've ever done. It's a good goal. It'll stretch them a little, but not much.

The types of goals that I want you to set for yourself are the stretch goals, the amazing goals, the world-class goals, the goals that arouse the fire, the juice, and the inspiration that will make you grow out of your comfort zone.

When you make the goal impossible, you stop working from your present knowledge and assumptions. You start opening to new ideas that will cause you to stretch and behave your way into your big goal.

Let me ask another question: if you wanted to grow your profits by ten times, how would you do it? The answer to this question will get you to start thinking much bigger; it will also eliminate many possible strategies and allow you to focus only on a few. *Less is more*: I want that tattooed on your brain.

The goal always determines the framework from which we operate. The only way to improve the present is by improving the future, so start with decision-making. Commit to your goal with every cell of your body, and divorce yourself from the outcome such that it would be impossible for it *not* to be achieved. And every day, make the decision that every day is day one.

Avoid the Cycle of Doom

What keeps people from achieving their goals and setting big, stretch goals? They're letting their results control them. Every time you let results control you, you think the same thoughts that you've always thought, which create the same feelings that you've always felt, which cause the same actions that you've always taken, which produce the same results. This is the fulfilling cycle of doom.

Your goal demands that you grow. It demands that you be disciplined. It demands that you raise your standards and be willing to fail as your future self rather than succeeding as your present self. Letting current results control how you set goals keeps you in the fulfilling cycle of doom, and your dream will die away. As we've seen, it's the definition of insanity: doing the same thing over and over and expecting different results.

When the program stays in control, nothing changes. Your goal will demand that you upgrade your thinking, your standards, and your identity in order to be in vibrational alignment with that goal.

In the previous chapter on identity, I discussed the importance of accepting and rejecting ideas from your future self and your goal achieved. Your future self already knows how to do it. I want you to only accept ideas that are in harmony with the person who's achieved your goal. Any ideas that are not in harmony with this person should be rejected within a millisecond.

To become what you want, you must overcome the old you. You have to kill off the old you to bring the new you to life. As we've seen, the side effect is discomfort. But discomfort is a great sign: it's showing you that you're on the right path.

To achieve a big goal, you only need to improve 1 percent every day. When you compound that percentage over ninety days, the game changes. When I'm working with my elite clients, I always work backward with them. I share with them that this process is going to be easy if they will simplify their lives. Simplicity scales and complexity fails.

I want you to imagine that five days a week you commit to creating three wins every day. Compound that over ninety days and you have 194½ wins. What do you think your results are going to be over ninety days if you have 194½ wins? I like simplifying everything in my clients' minds, because goal achievement happens by exact law.

Commit to creating three wins every day.

Once we get out of our own way and start mastering the simple things, results compound dramatically. Entrepreneur Jim Rohn said that success is achieved through small, consistent daily disciplines, not through large, infrequent efforts. I agree. Small efforts create big results. By the same token, the little mistakes, the little procrastinations, compounded over time create disastrous results.

Your goal will require you to be very intentional with your thinking. You must think, feel, and act like the person who takes massive action each day. This is a great question to trigger yourself: what action am I *not* taking because of discomfort? The answer to this question will tell you how badly you want to achieve your aim.

The bridge between imagination and result is action, and I want you to take inspired action. Inspiration is "in spirit." It's invisible, but you can feel it. Involve yourself emotionally with the outcome as if it is already done, and act every day on creating your three wins.

But there is no action without discipline. Discipline is critical to action. You have to make action into a disciplined activity. When you do, you will start stacking win after win, which, compounded over months, will create massive results. If time passes between awareness and action, that is procrastination. If you say, "I know I have to do this," but you don't, the enemy in your mind—your ego, the old self— has beaten you, and you procrastinate.

How do you avoid procrastination? You do everything right now. Do it now. *Do it now* will change your life. About twenty years ago, when I was failing considerably, my back was against the wall. I had left my job, and I was getting married. Three weeks later, I was forced to change. This philosophy of "do it now" changed my results overnight. I started behaving in my new way before I was ready, and all of a sudden the results changed. In my first month, I increased my income by $10,000 a month. Within three months, I increased it by $25,000 a month.

This philosophy of "do it now" created a quantum leap in my life. Make doing it now your number one discipline for achieving your goal. When you do, you will develop perseverance, and you will stop overthinking. By acting on your ideas, you'll see immediate results, and you'll implement this strategy for the rest of your life, as I've done for the past twenty years.

Keep your goal in your mind and come from the assumption that it is impossible to fail. The person who is divorced from the outcome and is coming from the goal thinks only about how they can achieve it. Your results have not changed yet, but a conscious person who understands the goal achievement process never lets results control them. They use their higher faculties—their memory, perception, will, and intuition—and their imagination accepts the idea: *I am happy and grateful that I have achieved my worthy goal of turning my annual income into my monthly income.*

Make your own goal into a magnificent obsession by repeatedly emotionalizing it and thinking about it over and over. The repetition will eventually turn that goal into a desire. Once it's a desire, it's a done deal, because at that point, it becomes a desire in the universal subconscious mind.

I understand if you're having a hard time connecting the dots in this line of thinking, but I always use my mentor's philosophy: understand the laws of the universe. Implanting the desire into your subconscious mind releases energy and causes you to act. At the same time, it alters your vibration, and the whole universe conspires on your behalf to make your desire a reality.

Your vibration changes your actions. Your actions in turn dictate what you attract, so the image must manifest in results. Radically accept the idea that this goal is done. You would not have the goal if it were not meant to be fulfilled now.

Now I want to get into the six phases of goal creation:

1. Who am I? I'm a spiritual being living in a physical body. There's no limit to what I can achieve.
2. Where am I now? Where are my current results?
3. Where am I going? What do I really want more than anything else?
4. Here is what goal achievement turns into: the most fulfilling processes of your life are the critical choices, the decisions you make when you're acting on ideas right away, creating three wins every day, and thinking, feeling, and acting as the person who's already achieved their goal.
5. Can this goal be accomplished, and accomplished well? If one person can create great wealth, so can you. If one person can create great health, we know it can be done. If one person can do a thing, so can you.
6. The last of the six phases of goal creation is this: Am I willing to pay the price? Am I willing to pay the price of persisting in the desired state even when I don't see the results? Am I willing to pay the price of raising my standards? Am I willing to pay the price of taking action before I know whether I'm good enough to take the action?

The end result will be amazing, but as we've seen, getting out of your comfort zone is essential to achieving world-class goals. That means making the move before you're ready.

Understand that creation is already finished. What you want is already here—on its own frequency. Think of the iPhone before the iPhone existed. That idea already existed, but Steve Jobs connected with it to make it a reality. All you have to do is get on the frequency of what you want.

Your job is to meet the goal halfway. Lean into it and take yourself into the future. Your choices and decisions have to be emanating

> **Six Phases of Goal Creation**
>
> 1. Who am I?
> 2. Where am I now?
> 3. Where am I going?
> 4. Acting on ideas right away.
> 5. Can this goal be accomplished?
> 6. Am I willing to pay the price?

from the person who's already achieved that goal. That's how you meet your goal halfway.

The degree to which you are all-in reflects your commitment to your goal. If you're starting and stopping, you're all-out. You can't be 90 percent in. If you're 90 percent in, you're a 100 percent out.

All-in means that in your mind, you have already achieved the outcome. Once again, you've radically accepted the idea. Now you're working from the goal by skipping levels, by making decisions as the person who's already achieved it.

Here is where the future self framework is your best accountability partner. From this moment on, you make every decision from the goal already achieved. Every attitude is coming from your most prosperous frame of mind. You're looking only for the good in everything. You build your standards one at a time, and you think, feel, and act as the person who's already achieved the goal. Then you're going to pick the few disciplines your goal demands, and you're going to compound your applications of those disciplines over time. This future self framework will prevent you from drifting and align you with the person you want to become.

Since goals are activated with imagination, I want you to create disciplined imagination. With disciplined imagination, you're seeing only what you would see had you achieved your goal. This enables you to enter into the spirit of the goal. It improves your focus. Imagination is the language of the soul. It will take you everywhere and anywhere you want to go, and it will give you anything you want.

Your current results will show you how you've been using your imagination. But what else is magical about imagination? Imagination causes you to act.

Let's go over the most simple process for goal achievement. It has three rules:

1. You have to fuse with it. You become one with it. Everything you do is aligned with the goal. You're married to the goal and the goal is married to you.
2. You create identity-based behaviors from the goal. Early in this chapter, I said the goal determines the framework and processes that you must implement. What are some examples of identity-based behaviors? Behaving before you're ready. Leaving everybody much better off than you found them. You act on ideas right away. You do it now. These are examples of identity-based behaviors.
3. You're process-driven. You commit to three goal-achieving activities and three wins every day. This framework—fusing with the goal, creating your identity-based behaviors from the goal and taking three to six goal-achieving activities every day—compounded over ninety days, will create massive results.

Let's make your hours epic. I tell my clients to eliminate distraction. I have them work on sprints of thirty, sixty, and ninety minutes throughout their day.

Why? Because most people are working eight to ten hours in distracted time, when there's no productivity. When you work your goal-achieving activities in shorter sprints, with breaks in between, you're going to be more productive than you've ever been.

You have to get to know which sprint works for you. I do a lot of thirty- and forty-five-minute sprints. That's what works for me. I don't do a lot of sixty- or ninety-minute sprints because I'm not as effective then. Focus on your future self framework and doing your sprints from your future self. It's the quality of the work, not the quantity, that counts. Five great hours a day, compounded over years, will create a world-class life.

It's important to use leverage to reach your goals. What can you leverage? You could leverage other people's experience and strategies. You could leverage your old mistakes. You leverage the 80 percent of your low-income activities and give them to people on your team, outsource them, or completely eliminate them, while you work only on your highest-income, your top 20 percent, activities. In this way you can create freedom.

Introducing the Three-by-Four Formula

I want to close this chapter with a framework that will keep you from getting distracted and will create quantum leaps every ninety days. I call it the *three-by-four formula*. This is a ninety-day transformation plan.

The Three-by-Four Formula

For ninety days, commit to:

1. Holding yourself to three standards.
2. Carrying out three disciplines.
3. Performing three actions.
4. Tracking three wins.

---

1. Write your goal at the top of a sheet of paper, and under it write three *standards*. What three standards are you going to implement for the next ninety days? Work only on these standards. They could be, for example, beating your personal best every day. Or controlling your thinking. Perhaps refusing to let anything on the outside control you, or holding yourself up to an enormous self-image.
2. Then write out *disciplines*. What three disciplines does your goal demand? They could be upgrading your attitude, leadership, or thinking. Commit to working only on those three disciplines for the next ninety days.

3. Then write down three *actions* to be performed every day. If your goals are in sales, actions could be selling, getting out of your comfort zone, and calling prospects that you would never call before. Maybe you're contacting somebody that you've never contacted because you were afraid that they wouldn't give you the time or day or would simply say no.
4. Then you track three *wins*, such as showing up with confidence, earning two sales, and executing new ideas.

If you commit to executing the three-by-four formula and apply this five days a week for ninety days, it is going to change the game for you. You'll see why goal achievement happens so effortlessly.

Write out your three-by-four plan daily to remind yourself, and execute it without negotiating with yourself. You focus only on your three standards, your three disciplines, your three actions, and three wins.

This three-by-four formula will be a game changer in your life.

Goal achievement is an art. It's bringing energy from one frequency to the next. To create a world-class life, you have to have goals that are worthy of you rather than your being worthy of them. I want you to form stretch goals that will demand that you grow.

Key Points in This Chapter
- You can set and achieve world-class goals.
- Goals must be big, stretching, and inspiring enough to force personal growth and transformation.
- Achieving world-class goals requires a fundamental shift in mindset, identity, and daily habits and actions.
- The goal achievement process involves radical acceptance of the goal as already achieved, making it a magnificent obsession, and taking daily disciplined actions in alignment with your future self who has achieved the goal.
- Work in sprints of thirty, sixty, and ninety minutes.
- Follow the three-by-four formula: set three standards, three disciplines, three daily actions, and three daily wins.

CHAPTER 8

Discipline: The Key to Quantum Leaps

Discipline is not only the key to quantum leaps, it's a prerequisite for creating a life of freedom. When I was struggling, I was a great starter, but a terrible finisher. Let me tell you how I went from being a great starter with no follow-through to living a life of freedom.

When I was first starting to work with Bob Proctor, he said, "Arash, to create what you want, you need great discipline."

"We might as well stop, because I have terrible discipline," I said. "I'm a great starter and a terrible finisher."

He laughed.

"What's so funny?" I asked.

"You remind me of me. You're starting and stopping only because you've never been taught the rules of success, and you've never gotten the proper direction."

As I've already indicated, I've discovered that discipline is not about doing a hundred things: it's about doing a few things a hundred times. Moreover, discipline does not consist of the activities as such. It's disciplining the mind by accepting and rejecting ideas and creating the deliberate habit of follow-through.

Successful people do things that unsuccessful people are not willing to do. Winners are prepared to do what they don't want to do. Losers are not willing to do what they don't want to do.

Many people miss the key point of programming, which I explained in an earlier chapter. You can't program yourself for only a couple days a week: you have to do it every day. You get rewarded by what you consistently repeat.

We become what we repeatedly do. Habits are the only difference between those who are crushing it and those who are not making it happen.

The highest level of mastery is discipline. Discipline is mixed into everything we do: building our standards, changing our programming, taking action, and building a new self-image. We will never outperform the old story we have about ourselves.

Many people don't understand the importance of stories, but they are self-fulfilling prophecies for our lives. Everything extraordinary that we have done has had a great story associated with it. The mind takes the event, ascribes meaning to it, puts it into a story, and gives it to the brain, which turns it into a belief. So you will want to use discipline to upgrade your stories.

Discipline is a constant human awareness of the need for action and a conscious act to implement that action. If awareness and execution occur at the same time, we master discipline. If we wait, we're in procrastination.

Discipline is not about living a life of restriction. It's about living a life of freedom. It's about harmony. Think about how good you feel about yourself when you are disciplined.

Discipline is not about living a life of restriction. It's about living a life of freedom.

Discipline is especially important for transformation because all forms of disciplines affect each other. Good disciplines effect more good disciplines. Bad disciplines bring about more bad disciplines.

Discipline is delayed gratification in action. Delayed gratification is a game changer. It is seeing the bigger picture. High-performing achievers, real peak performers, are obsessed with delayed gratification. They know that the continued practice of a few disciplines, compounded over time, will create big results. Low and average achievers fail to see this truth.

It takes discipline to conquer the limiting voices in our mind. We have an enemy in our minds, although no one at a young age is taught about it. It's the voice that says you're not good enough. You may have tried to conquer this defeatist voice before and failed, but when you develop discipline, you will.

It takes discipline to be honest with ourselves. It takes discipline to accept and reject ideas from the perspective of our future self, and it takes discipline to create new habits. The greatest value of discipline is that it builds self-worth and self-esteem dramatically. Think about the last time you really pushed yourself out of your comfort zone. How did you feel? Every time I'm out of my comfort zone, I know I'm transforming my identity. You feel so good when you're out of your comfort zone. That's the power of discipline.

If time passes between awareness and action, that is procrastination. How do we avoid procrastination? It's always with discipline. We give ourselves a command and we do it. When I was struggling, my back was against the wall; the only difference between where I was and where I became in thirty days was this one habit of discipline. Everything I did, I did it right away. I learned this from an indirect mentor of mine, W. Clement Stone, a businessman and author of New Thought books. He wrote a powerful book with Napoleon Hill called *Success through a Positive Mental Attitude,* and he kept reinforcing how much doing it *now* changed his life.

That's all I did. Everything I did for thirty days was do it now, do it now, do it now. The results in my life transformed dramatically. Test it for yourself. When you test something, you'll know and have your own visceral experience. But understand, discipline is what causes us to move into action. Discipline is the key to action.

When you intentionally discipline your thinking, you will think and act like the person you want to be, and your actions will be much bolder. Failure to discipline your thinking will affect every area of your life, including your actions, which in turn affect your results, your philosophy, and identity. When you build up your discipline, your actions change as a result.

If you work backward, what are results? They are a manifestation of actions. These are a manifestation of subconscious thinking, which in turn is a manifestation of conscious thinking. When you resolve to think, feel, and act, and make decisions from your goal already achieved, that's discipline in action.

Know in every cell of your being that you are going to the top.

I encourage you right now to know in every cell of your being that you are going to the top, and I want you to believe in yourself before the results happen. I want you to believe right now that if one person can do it, you can do it. If one person can create great wealth, so can you. Now ask yourself what actions you are not taking because of discomfort. This will tell you an enormous amount about your programming.

Your actions will always tell you how badly you really want your goal. They will also tell you how truly and authentically you believe. Action is the fundamental key to success. It is not good enough to have the knowledge and talent, to just speak the words. It's about using that knowledge, working the ideas, and unleashing your talent.

Develop the ability to act. The time to act is when the idea is burning in your mind and the emotion is strong. Make it a priority to *do it now*. I promise you, that is a seven- and eight-figure habit. When you do this, you're upgrading your standard, you're mixing it with discipline, and you're going to create world-class results.

You will see immediate results by acting on your idea. The great thing is that you will implement this strategy for the rest of your life. Personal action is critical to creating the results you want. Your results always manifest your actions.

Recently I was talking to a client, who said, "You know, Arash, I'm having trouble with discipline. My day gets away from me, and I get torn in this direction and that direction."

Discipline: The Key to Quantum Leaps

"Discipline is not your issue," I replied, "focus is. You're getting distracted. I'm going to give you something to do. If you do it for the next sixty days, it will change the game."

"OK, what is it?"

"Every night, I want you to write out three nonnegotiables that you're going to accomplish the next day. Just three. I want you to accomplish three big things, so even if you get distracted, you come back. I want you to do the hardest thing first, because if you start your day doing the hardest thing, you build confidence. Now you have momentum working for you. Now you're disciplining your environment."

I want you to be so in love with the actions you're taking that you know the outcome before you start. That's inspired action with swagger, with confidence, with detachment. That's when your results are going to chase you. Just remember, do it now. You must act now. You cannot act in the past. Dismiss your past, because your past is dead. Release it completely from your mind. The magic always lies in the momentum.

The start is the hardest part.

There's a great quote by the Hall of Fame football coach Don Shula, who said that the start is the hardest part. So how do you start the momentum?

1. Set clear goals that inspire you.
2. Break your goals down into daily action steps that would be impossible *not* to take.
3. When your goal is clear, your focus sharpens.
4. You need a big *why*, which pulls you out of the comfort of inaction.
5. Every time you take an action step, you build greater and greater self-respect.

Key Points in This Chapter

- The key to quantum leaps in life is discipline, which is the foundation for creating true freedom. Discipline is not about doing 100 things, but rather doing a few things 100 times.
- Discipline the mind by accepting and rejecting ideas as appropriate and creating the habit of follow-through.
- Successful people are willing to do what unsuccessful people are not willing to do.
- Discipline is mixed into everything we do, from building our standards to changing our programming and self-image.
- Our stories and beliefs shape our reality, so upgrading our stories through discipline is crucial.
- To create an absolute transformation, you must have a powerful *why* that will drive you through adversity.
- Discipline builds self-worth and self-esteem. The habit of doing it now can dramatically transform results in just thirty days.
- Action is the fundamental key to success. Act on your ideas while they are burning hot within you.

CHAPTER 9

Money Is a Mirror

My mindset and identity shift created my first financial quantum leap. I remember vividly when I finally cracked the wealth code, when I stopped living paycheck to paycheck and no longer had the pressure of debt. Then I started asking myself about the biggest shifts that I made. They were never financial. My shifts led to financial shifts, but in the end, it was always a matter of upgrading my programming and changing my thermostat.

Let's talk about money. Most people do not understand the rules of money, and that's why they're not earning a lot of money. Transformation happens when you commit to growth. You take bold action. You're relentless in your action, you are relentless in your thinking, and you refuse to stay the same. When your transformation becomes sacred, your personal growth becomes sacred.

You are one decision away right now from living the life you want to live. That decision is committing to a big goal that inspires you and doing what you love and loving what you do.

Wealth is a spiritual journey and a spiritual idea. You have to learn how to operate on a higher spiritual plane. There is no reason for people to struggle to get to breakthrough. You can skip levels. I will show you, right now, the greatest idea for activating wealth in your life: *make every decision from the wealth that you desire.* Refuse to think about how it's going to happen day in and day out. If you make decisions as the person who's already achieved that type of wealth, opportunities are going to chase you down.

Nobody earns a lot of money until they decide to, so you have to decide that you're going to earn and turn your annual income into your monthly income. That's a big idea for a lot of people.

I remember I was sitting in a seminar in Scottsdale, Arizona, with Bob Proctor, before he became my mentor. I was in the front row. He put up a slide that took me on a completely different thought trip. The slide said, "You can create your own economy."

Make every decision from the wealth that you desire.

At that point, I stopped listening. All I could think about was what I could do to create my own economy. The next slide said, "You can turn your annual income into your monthly income." You can imagine where I was at this point.

I was still working at a job that I didn't enjoy. I had been studying personal development and success philosophies for three years and hadn't created any results. And then Bob hit me with those two slides. I left that room, and unbeknownst to me, this idea started using me. I kept thinking about how could I turn my annual income into my monthly income. How I could create my own economy.

I fell in love with the questions about this idea, and then I committed to creating that before I was even ready. I made the decision and started studying the most prominent teachers. I hired Bob Proctor as my mentor, and everything changed.

One idea can change your life.

One idea changed my life, and then it became a bunch of ideas.

I want you to understand that your divine right is to be wealthy. That is God-given. God doesn't just touch a few people on the shoulder while everybody else struggles. That's not how it works. It all depends on the decisions we make, the habits we create, the standards we cultivate, and the actions that we follow through on. We only go as far as our thinking goes.

Look at your current money blueprint—at what you're earning right now. That is your money blueprint, telling you a story. If you love the story, keep doing the same thing. If you want to transform the story, make a decision: create a significant income goal that is going to cause you to grow and grow. Watch the synchronicities that start happening as you upgrade your programming and your identity, build your standards, and follow the goal achievement process that I've taught you.

Money comes from conquering yourself. You can create your own economy just as I did (and I've done it multiple times). I'm no different from you. If I can do it, you can absolutely do it. I love this quote by Wallace D. Wattles, author of *The Science of Getting Rich*, published in 1910. Back then—and it's true today—he wrote, "The amount of wealth a person receives is directly related to the clarity of their goals, the unwavering commitment to achieving them, their level of belief in their ability to succeed, and the depth of their appreciation for what they already have in life."

Let's dissect this quote so you can implement it. My paraphrase: The riches you receive will be in exact proportion to the definiteness of your vision. The clarity of your goals: what do you really want more than anything else? What is your number one goal? "The unwavering commitment" to achieving your goals: how unwavering are you? Your "level of belief in your ability to succeed": steady faith in seeing what you want, believing in the incredible. Your subconscious mind will give you exactly what you give it.

Appreciation for what you already have in life: that's gratitude. What is the depth of your gratitude? Gratitude is the vibration of abundance. Create a disciplined gratitude practice, because gratitude is where wealth lives.

Ask yourself about your relationship with money. Do you think money is easy to earn, or would you say, "I don't even know how in the world I would make a lot of money"?

Another prominent question is whether you feel you deserve money, because you will never create something in your life that you do not feel worthy of.

Are your actions and behaviors congruent with a state of abundance? Am you constantly thinking about what's missing? Are you in lack? Are you only thinking about *how* money is going to come? Your beliefs about money have to be congruent with your financial goal.

Opening your heart means releasing resistance.

Opening your heart means releasing resistance. Every time you experience resistance, I want you to act on it. Think about some of the things you believe. Think about what you believe is possible financially. Are you believing it because it's true, or are you just believing it because you believe it's true? Most people never question their assumptions: their beliefs are always harmonize with their past experiences and current programming.

What if I told you your entire income and cash flow depends on one thing: your relationship with money?

Think about this: If you went on a date with money and money were sitting across from you and you said, "You're the root of all evil. Only bad people ever have it, and they abuse it," would money ever go out on a second date with you? The answer is obviously no.

Most people want to create more money, but they have such an unhealthy relationship with it that they're constantly creating double-binding messages. Napoleon Hill wrote a great essay about this subject called "The Big Money." He said money is shy and timid: it must be attracted by the person we become. He said poverty is bold and ruthless: it's easy to attract.

I'm going to share with you a technique that changed my relationship with money. It's a quote from Joseph Murphy's book *The Power of Your Subconscious Mind*: "I like money, I love it. I use it wisely, constructively, and judiciously. Money is constantly circulating in my life. I release it with joy and it returns to me multiplied in wonderful ways. Money flows to me in avalanches of abundance. I use it for only good. I am grateful for the good and riches of my mind."

I understood that I had so much scarcity in my heart, I had so much lack and limitation, that I had to change my relationship with money. Once I started learning the rules of money, I would write out this affirmation every day five times, and then I would record it on my phone and listen to it ten minutes a day. The repetition of writing and recording started changing my relationship with money. Then I said to myself, "I'm going to become every word of this statement," and that's how I created a completely different relationship with money.

Right now, if you are filled with scarcity in your heart, if you are struggling financially, I promise you it is based on beliefs about your relationship with money. Write out the affirmation above five times every day, read it aloud, record it, and listen to it ten minutes a day. Then start seeing money circulating in your life. Every time you get a bill in the mail, start seeing it as a check. Start spending $10,000 in your mind. When a nice car drives by, say, "I can pay for that."

That's how you're going to do it. You're going to change your relationship with money over time. If you see money as stressful, scarce, or hard to get, you'll always unconsciously push it away. But if you see money as a tool, as an extension flowing easily from the value you create, you'll naturally attract it and multiply it.

Success isn't just about earning money. It's about mastering the mindset that allows wealth to grow effortlessly. Change your relationship with money, and you will change everything around wealth. Your relationship with money is one of the most important factors in your success. The late motivational speaker Zig Ziglar said, "Money isn't the most important thing in life, but it's reasonably close to oxygen on the 'got to have it' scale. Without money, we can't eat. Without eating, there is no life."

Once again, what is your expectation, attitude, and relationship with money? The way you think, feel, and act around money directly impacts how much of it flows into your life and how well you manage it.

To cultivate a successful relationship with money, I've created a framework that would make it impossible for you *not* to increase your wealth.

> **Eight Principles of Money**
>
> 1. Decide to be wealthy.
> 2. Shift from a scarcity consciousness to an abundance consciousness.
> 3. Detach emotionally.
> 4. Respect money.
> 5. Expand your capacity to receive.
> 6. Value over hustle.
> 7. Normalize wealth.
> 8. Give without fear.

Eight Principles of Money

1. **Decide to be wealthy.** Success with money starts with a decision—not a wish, but a firm commitment to becoming financially empowered, no matter what it takes.
2. **Shift from a scarcity consciousness to an abundance consciousness.** Money isn't something to chase or fear. It's a tool that flows in response to value. Stop seeing it as limited, and start seeing opportunities everywhere.
3. **Detach emotionally.** Money is neutral. It's not good or bad; it just is. Don't let fear, guilt, or anxiety control your financial decisions. Instead, make empowered, strategic choices.
4. **Respect money.** If you respect money, it will stay and grow. Track it. Invest wisely, and always know where it's going.
5. **Expand your capacity to receive.** Many people subconsciously block wealth because of limiting beliefs such as, "I don't deserve this" or "Making money is hard." Rewrite those beliefs to match the level of wealth you desire.
6. **Value over hustle.** Value creation is always greater than hustle. Money always follows value. Instead of just working harder, focus on creating more impact, solving bigger problems, improving your skill set and serving at a higher level.

7. **Normalize wealth.** Get comfortable with the idea of wealth. You don't even think about it, just like breathing. Surround yourself with people who have a healthy, abundant relationship with money. The more you see wealth as normal and comfortable, the easier it becomes to attract.
8. **Give without fear.** Generosity is circulation and signals confidence, abundance, and opulence. When you give freely without depletion, when you give unconditionally and never worry if your gift is ever going to be returned, you open the doors for more money and opulence to flow back to you.

If you understand these eight principles, you will change your relationship with money.

Wealth always flows in our life as we see ourselves bigger. That's the key to wealth. It's not the money itself: it's how we see ourselves. The magic is always in how we see ourselves. The currency for attracting what we want into our life is our thoughts. Every thought is a form of currency. Your energy is also a form of currency. I want you to have the energy of the goal that you want to accomplish, the energy of knowingness, the energy of detachment.

Never chase anything. Your income always reflects your identity, and you will never outearn your identity.

To understand money, we have to understand the law of compensation. Emerson wrote a phenomenal essay titled "Compensation," which I encourage you to read every day. He explores what he calls "the law of compensation." It states that we get paid in exact proportion to the service we render, depending on our ability to render that service and the need for it in the marketplace. The most important aspect of the law of compensation is our ability to provide that service.

In my workshops, I constantly focus on improving my ability to present. That's the law of compensation in action. When you are working in harmony with it, money will start flowing in your life. Customers will start knocking on your door, and abundance will chase you down. Service to many means greatness. Service to many also leads to great wealth.

Money is the greatest illusion. Most people are making every decision based on what they can afford in their bank account rather than what they want. When you make a decision, whether you have the money or not, your mind will focus on how. Money always comes as a result of the person you become. You will always attract it by your thinking, feelings, and actions. Money is a consciousness and it must be earned.

> Money always comes as a result
> of the person you become.

Money is a great servant, but a horrible master. Most people are slaves to money instead of having money as their slave. Again, ask yourself, what is your philosophy about money? Do you think it's easy to earn?

Why is philosophy so important? Because philosophy is our automatic belief system. Philosophy creates your standard. Your standard creates your story. Your story creates your identity, and your identity creates your results.

How to Improve Your Relationship with Money

How do you make money your friend? These are six ways to improve your relationship with money.

1. Journal for fifteen minutes a day on your money goal. Write out your financial goal at the top of a piece of paper and set a timer for fifteen minutes. During this time, write down as many ideas as you can. Don't judge the ideas. Some of them will be good; some of them will be bad. That's the point.

    When I started doing this years ago, I was creating a prosperity consciousness, even though I didn't know what I was doing.

> ### Six Ways to Improve Your Relationship with Money
> 1. Journal daily.
> 2. Read books on money philosophy.
> 3. Always keep money in your wallet.
> 4. Create an affirmation.
> 5. Be comfortable with the idea of money in your life.
> 6. Discipline your mind to build a wealth consciousness.

I discovered that when you think of ways you can make money, you're developing a healthy relationship with it.

2. Read books on money philosophy. The one that had the greatest impact on me is an older one by Raymond Charles Barker called *Money Is God in Action*. It's a very small pamphlet, but it's powerful.
3. Always keep money in your wallet. I don't care if you spend it, but the more your subconscious sees hundred-dollar bills in your wallet or purse, the more you'll start seeing it flow into your life. Give, give, give. Give compliments; give whatever you can. Mentally spend $10,000 a day. Whenever you see a bill in the mail, see it as a check. This sounds silly, but test it for yourself.
4. Create an affirmation that you say to yourself a hundred times a day: *I'm so happy and grateful now that money comes to me through both expected and unexpected sources.*

    Say it as if you're singing a song. Constant repetition will rewire your programming.
5. Love money, and be comfortable with the idea of money in your life. Years ago, when I was struggling, I went to dinner with a very affluent individual. I asked him, "What's the trick around money?"

    "No one has money until they're comfortable with the idea of it," he replied.

    "I'm comfortable. I want to earn more."

    "How much do you have?"

    "Not much."

"So you're not comfortable with the idea."

I walked away thinking about what this gentleman told me. I was the definition of a double-binding message: I wanted more, but I was coming from lack, so I was never comfortable with the idea of money. I had to build a new money story for myself. I kept working on it, day in, day out, and it started changing little by little. Then it began to change rapidly.

6. Discipline your mind to build a wealth consciousness. Using the example that I've been employing throughout this book, let's say your goal is earning in a month what you used to earn in a year. You are constantly reaffirming every morning throughout the day: *I'm so happy and grateful now that I'm earning a hundred thousand or more every month.*

Yet you may not see the results. Why? If constant repetition changes the programming, why are you not seeing a change of results? It's always because you're sending out a double-binding message. You say, "I want money," but the rest of the day, your attention is on the outside results: on what's missing. Whenever you put attention on outside results, the situation goes back to what you've been getting already. Even though you want more money, you're coming from a poverty consciousness that triggers worry, doubt, and fear.

Wake up. Discipline your mind to build a wealth consciousness, and use your higher faculties. Think only about what you want. Your every thought will be like that of the person who earns $100,000 a month. Every emotional state will be excitement and pride in what you're doing. You already have peace of mind. You are training yourself and operating from the version of who you want to become. Every decision, every thought, every feeling, and every action is coming from that person. Over time, this will alter your vibration and create opportunities, which you're going to act on. Once you change your programming, the action happens automatically, and the results change.

I'm asking you to create exponential growth, so that you go from lack to abundance. Rewrite, renew, and rewire your programming.

From this moment on, focus on creating a high prosperity consciousness. Once again, a great way to do this is to create an affirmation: *money comes to me through both expected and unexpected sources.*

Your mind is a garden. What are you planting in it? Are you planting what you want? Are you planting your goal, or are you planting what you don't want? Whatever you plant grows. You can grow poison, you can grow abundance, you can grow lack, or you can grow wealth. What are you planting in your garden? Do not plant bad seed in it.

Study chapter 4 on programming abundance for a scarcity mindset. The cause of poverty is thinking poverty thoughts. A poverty consciousness causes a person to see, feel, and hear lack and limitation. You'll hear it in their language: "I never have enough money." How much are you earning? They never want to share what they're earning. They're constantly talking about gas prices, interest rates, the economy. This individual is obsessed on what they *don't* want. Lack and limitation are all they talk about. As a result, their thoughts, feelings, actions—the seeds they're sowing—are those of poverty, so that's all they're going to see in their lives.

On the other hand, a person with a wealth consciousness demands abundance. They're asking the world for more than they can even imagine. They're constantly and consistently expecting more. They act on ideas right away. They do it now; they take full responsibility and ownership. They're the only problem they have and the only solution they have. They know that there's an unlimited supply. There's enough to go around for everybody. They are relentlessly thinking of abundance. They loathe being around people who are constantly focused on problems, lack, and limitation. Those with a wealth consciousness are always circulating money. They understand the law of circulation: that whatever they put out, they're going to get back tenfold.

Most people are creating from a place of not having money: they're coming from a wanting state and subconsciously blocking themselves. You have to create from a place of worthiness: "I already have it: I'm so grateful for the abundance that keeps flowing into my life." When you get to the point where you have the idea in your subconscious mind, the universe will realize you're out of the way, and wealth will be drawn to you. It's never about *how*. It's always about *who do I have to become?* Whom can I model? Who's already created what I want? A wealthy vibration has no lack. There's no such thing as being 50 percent in a wealthy vibration. It's either 100 percent or zero.

Remember the rules of money that we have to follow: love, speed, and do it now. Act on ideas. Act before you're ready. When you follow these rules, you'll start looking for opportunities everywhere. Ask yourself, where are my acres of diamonds right now? Where are the opportunities in my job or my business that I haven't been seeing? When you start looking for them, avalanches of abundance will start coming in.

Key Points in This Chapter
- Wealth is a spiritual journey and requires upgrading your programming and identity.
- The key to wealth is not the money, but how you see yourself.
- Thoughts and energy are the currency for attracting what you desire.
- The law of compensation states that we get paid in proportion to the value we provide and our ability to provide that value.
- Making decisions based on what you can afford rather than what you desire is a limiting mindset. Make decisions from the perspective of the person who has already achieved their desired wealth.
- Cultivating a healthy relationship with money involves practices like journaling, reading books on money philosophy, giving generously, and using affirmations.
- Overcoming a scarcity mindset and developing an abundance consciousness is essential for attracting wealth.

CHAPTER 10

Don't Be Fooled by Circumstances

Your current circumstances are not your destiny. They do not reflect your true potential. They reflect your past thinking, decisions, and actions. Circumstances are feedback, not a forecast.

Most people live as if their circumstances are permanent. They let their bank account, their business results, their body, or their environment dictate how they feel, what they believe, and how they show up. That's the ultimate trap. Circumstances scream limitations, but your inner power whispers possibilities.

It's easy to let circumstances control our lives. We've been trained to believe in physicality: "I'll believe it when I see it." The truth is, you'll see it *once you believe it.*

If you only focus on what you see, you'll stay stuck where you are. Real power comes when you see beyond what is and act from what can be. Winners don't trust circumstances. They trust their vision, their goals, their decisions, and their ability to create change from within. They know circumstances are temporary and will bend to the will of someone who refuses to accept them as final.

I created the first best year of my life in 2008, when there was a housing crisis and it was the worst economy in the U.S. that I'd ever experienced. Yet I created the best results I'd ever had up to that point. How was that possible?

Most people let the outside—that is, other people's version of the economy—control them. The real winners put their foot on the gas while the people who are playing it safe put their foot on the brake. I put my foot on the gas in 2008. Everybody was telling me how bad the economy was, but I didn't accept that idea.

You've got to decide what kind of economy you want to create. You've got to decide that you're going to multiply your income significantly regardless of circumstances.

Decide what kind of economy you want to create.

In this chapter, I'll show you how to break free from the illusion of circumstances, how to stop letting your environment control your mindset, and how to develop the internal leadership that makes you unstoppable regardless of what's going on around you.

I got a call one morning from a great client of mine, Jake. He called me from Japan and said, "This huge deal is blowing up. This will be a great hit to my business."

I asked Jake, "What do you really want?"

"I want to re-form this deal and make it into a win-win for one year."

For a year, I had been coaching Jake on not allowing circumstances to control him or his thinking.

I told him all I wanted him to do. I said, "Jake, I want you to be obsessed with the outcome. It will happen. We will create a win-win for you."

For one year, Jake did exactly what I told him to do, and two months ago he closed the deal and saved a multimillion-dollar deal for his company. His example shows that who you are becoming is more important than who you've been.

Understand this truth: your future depends not on yesterday, but what you do today. Refuse to let outside circumstances fool you. Your future depends, not on the past, but on what you do day in and day out. Every day is day one. Start right now and grow into whatever your heart desires.

I want this idea to drive your thinking and your emotional state. Your actions come from your heart's desire. As I've already emphasized, this will demand that you step up and out of your comfort zone.

If you are struggling with letting the circumstances control you, I suggest that you discipline yourself to follow the 1 percent rule. Determine that you will not allow circumstances to control you. Refuse to let the outside control the inside. Instead, just get 1 percent better every day.

Your goal is your driving force. It sets your life in motion. I want your goal to be huge in your mind, and I want you to assume that your success is guaranteed. I love this quote from the Roman emperor and philosopher Marcus Aurelius: "If a thing is humanly possible, consider it to be within your reach." In other words, if one person can create great success, so can you. If one person can overcome their circumstances, so can you. If your goal is worthy of you, it will require you to overcome adversity.

I encourage you to lean into adversity. As soon as you face adversity, take action right away. That is your weapon; lean into it. The minute you hesitate is the minute adversity has won.

**If a thing is humanly possible,
consider it to be within your reach.**

When you start your day in your morning routine, decide right at the outset that you are betting on yourself today, that today is going to be your magnificent obsession. Set the intention that you will not allow circumstances to control you. I want you to keep betting on yourself, day in and day out. That action, compounded over time, creates massive transformation.

I want you to have the courage to go where the expectations are high. Every time you do, you're raising your standards. Our results always tell us what is going on inside of us. They're a compass of our lives. Don't run from your results. Sprint to your results. Get into the attitude that you can overcome whatever life may throwing at you.

To repeat a point I've made throughout this book, never let results dictate your thinking, because the minute you do, it controls your emotional state. Your emotional state in turn alters your vibration, and your vibration dictates what you attract.

You are now coming from your greatest competitive advantage, because 98 percent of the population are letting their circumstances dictate who they are. True transformation demands that you be bold. It demands that you accept ideas that you can't see with your physical eyes but which you know are really activating your life. With this realization, the result simply functions as feedback to allow you to correct course.

By contrast, letting results control you activates lack and limitation. It stops you from dreaming and going after what you truly want. It keeps you from transforming, breaking free, and welcoming breakthroughs into your life.

When you permit present results to control your thoughts, you cannot improve your income, your health, or your relationships. Don't let your emotions distract you from doing what needs to be done. Control your emotions so that they do not control you.

There's a great quote from the inspirational speaker and author Neville Goddard: "Truth is subjective and depends on the intensity of imagination, not on external facts." As I have been saying, facts are based on the past. Imagination is based on a bigger, bolder, better future.

Facts are based on the past. Imagination is based on a bigger, bolder, better future.

To create great wealth, you must know two things: where you are and where you're going. Those are the only two things you have to know. You want to fill in the identity gap, which is the gap between where you are and where you're going.

It is so simple and so obvious. Why, then, are so many people stuck? Because instead of focusing all their energy on their desired state, they spend it on letting outside circumstances keep reminding them of where they currently are.

When you make this paradigm shift, you change your life. This is a black-and-white concept. It does not matter how hard you work or how many hours you put in. If the program does not change, ultimately the results will remain the same from one year to the next. This is why most people live the same year over and over again for fifty years. When the program stays in control, nothing changes.

To transform, you have to stop allowing the circumstances to dictate your actions. If you do, they cause you to feel the same emotions that you've been feeling, which created the circumstances that cause you to think the same thoughts.

Let's look at results and work backward. Results justify our actions. Our actions are a manifestation of our subconscious programming. Our subconscious programming is a manifestation of our conscious thinking. That's why you must only accept ideas from what you really want—the result that you want to achieve—even though you don't see it with your physical eyes.

When you make your future a magnificent obsession and keep seeing what you want to see, feeling what you want to feel, and acting as the person who already has achieved your desired state, your circumstances will change.

But why do so many people choose ideas that produce results they don't want? Because they are obsessed with their circumstances, and they are not thinking.

I'm asking you to think differently. When you do, your belief is much stronger. And guess what? Your results change.

Now let's take a good look and remind yourself who you are. You are a spiritual being living in a physical body. You have infinite potential, and you've been endowed with a mind. The way you use that mind creates your environment.

Your conscious mind is your thinking mind. It's your educated mind. It's where your intellect resides. Your subconscious mind, on the other hand, is your powerhouse. It's your emotional mind. It's impersonal. It doesn't know what's good for you or what's bad. It only knows what your conscious mind supplies to it.

Your conscious mind can accept or reject any idea it chooses. You can choose any idea you want. I want you only to accept ideas that come from your goal and your future self. Reject any idea that opposes them. You can originate any idea in your conscious mind. Originate world-class ideas. Have a world-class image. Live a world-class life.

Your subconscious mind must accept the ideas it receives, so if you do not discipline yourself to accept or reject ideas, circumstances will create the ideas for you, along with your programming. Your subconscious mind cannot determine the difference between what's real and what's imagined. That's why I want you to let your imagination fly, open it up, and imagine you are living exactly how you want to live.

Every day is day one when you resolve to make every decision coming from the person who's already achieved your goal.

Many negative influences are coming from the outside, from social media, from people with small, scarcity mindsets. You have to guard your mind all day long. Your ability to accept and reject ideas throughout the day will transform you. It is your competitive advantage in the marketplace. In each second, with every thought that comes in, you can control the flow of thought energy, let it flow freely, either accept or reject, and improve your life by connecting it only with what you want.

With every thought that comes in, you can control the flow of thought energy.

Understand this: everything is a thought and is under your control. Your ability to think is the highest form of creation.

If we don't discipline ourselves, I promise you the world will do it for us, and most people are letting the outside discipline what is going on inside. I want you to create great subjective control, whereby you decide whether or not you're going to accept an idea, a thought, or a vision for yourself.

> **Reframing**
>
> 1. At the end of the day, rethink your day hour by hour from the beginning.
> 2. For each hour, ask yourself if you had any limiting thoughts.
> 3. If you didn't, go to the next hour.
> 4. Pick out times when you let outside circumstances control you or let somebody else bother you.
> 5. Imagine that situation, and imagine yourself choosing the exact opposite of what you were doing during the day.
> 6. Go through your day this way.

I will give you a powerful process that I practice every night. I teach it to all my elite clients. It's called *reframing*. At the end of your day, rethink your day hour by hour from the beginning. Start when you woke up, and go through the day. Ask yourself if you had any limiting thoughts. If you didn't, go to the next hour. Go hour by hour, then pick up times when you let outside circumstances control you or let somebody else bother you.

Now imagine that situation, and imagine yourself choosing the exact opposite of what you were doing during the day. Now you are no longer allowing the outside to control you. Every time you do this, you limit the impact of negative events and reactions on your subconscious mind. This powerful practice will only take you a couple minutes to do every night, but it is an absolute game changer.

Your mind and thoughts must operate on the same frequency as your goal. Ask what your goal demands. How would that person think? How would that person feel? Decide, "I'm going to feel that way. I'm going to feel excited. I'm going to feel fired up. I'm going to feel proud of myself. I'm going to have peace of mind. I'm going to act even before I'm ready."

It is crucial to develop great focus. Focus increases the amplitude of vibration. It is a mental muscle that gets you into the spirit of the good that you desire. The best tool for sharpening focus is personal responsibility. Say this: *I am the only problem I'm ever going to have, and I'm the only solution I'm ever going to have.* I want you to assume that your success is absolutely guaranteed. When you do that, everything's going to change.

> Say: "I am the only problem I'm ever going to have, and I'm the only solution I'm ever going to have."

The Power of Attitude

In order to keep the outside from controlling you, you have to understand the importance of attitude in your life.

Attitude changed my life. One day I was talking to my mentor, and I told him, "Bob, I'm stuck right now."

"Why are you stuck?"

"I'm not getting the results that I had been getting."

"So you're going to let the results control your thinking?"

I was doing the exact opposite of what I'm teaching you in this chapter.

Bob said, "I'm going to teach you a powerful lesson that my mentor taught me. Anybody can have a great attitude when things are going well. The true professionals in life have an even better attitude when things aren't going as well."

It was like a punch in my gut, and I devoted to two years to studying my attitude. Your results reflect your attitude. Your attitudes are a combination of your thoughts, feelings, and actions. Every thought that you have goes out into the universe, and the universe will create a boomerang of thoughts that are in harmony with that thought, and these turn into feelings.

Those feelings are then sent out into the universe. The universe will match those feelings exactly, which you put right back into your life. At that point your body will be in the vibration that causes you to act, that's in harmony with your thoughts and feelings. This is how you create results.

Our results are no more than our attitude. Attitude is a game changer. Constantly assume the feeling that you already have what you want. Well, guess what? That's attitude right there. I want you to have the most prosperous, positive mental attitude, where you're looking for the good in everything and you understand that success always leaves clues. You get to choose any idea you want. When the desire is strong, your goal will overtake your old self and your old programming. That's why your want has to be an obsession. At that point, everything changes.

What I want driving you is not your senses but your higher faculties, which are in your conscious mind: your memory, your perception, your will, your imagination, your intuition, and your reasoning. With these, you can tap into universal intelligence.

You let it happen. You don't force it: you *allow*. When you allow, you're working with the good of what you desire. You begin creating the life you want. You fall in love with the idea on a conscious level by seeing yourself as you would be. You connect with the love of your desire on an emotional level, and you see the dream manifest in your life.

Remind yourself: *Desire is my high-octane fuel. How would I feel if what I wanted is what I'm experiencing right now?* Feel those feelings beforehand—the excitement, the pride, the inspiration, the fire in your belly. Start right now. Grow into whatever your heart desires. Always have the standard that you love betting on yourself. When you do, everything changes.

Everything is a frequency, and everything is a vibration. Right now, you're reading these words. That is a frequency. What you're thinking is a frequency. Every thought has a frequency. You want to align yourself with the frequency of your goal. You can only do that when you decide to act *only* as the person who's already achieved your goal. You are no longer accepting results based on the outside world.

When you make decisions based on the evidence of the outside world, you just keep recreating your same environment, with same results as from what you've always been doing. But when you bet on yourself and you have the courage to say—even though you don't see it—"This is where I'm going," you give yourself a command. You make a definite, irrevocable decision: "This is what I'm creating. I am turning my annual income into my monthly income."

When your mind and thoughts operate on the same frequency as your goal, magic enters your life. But this can only happen when you knock down the brick wall of your paradigm. Once you make that irrevocably committed decision and consistently follow through on it, day in and day out, you will think and act like the person you want to become, and your results will change.

What you want is the only prerequisite for making a decision. You don't need to know how to do it. You could be struggling, but that has no bearing on you. When you want something badly enough, you will raise your standards and your discipline, and you will attract the good you desire.

This is why successful people make decisions so fast. They have always stayed focused on their goals and have been consistent in their efforts. Their will to carry through on their aim is relentless. Train yourself to act as your future self. Never allow any evidence from the outside to control your thinking.

Key Points in This Chapter

- Circumstances are not permanent: they do not reflect your true potential. They are feedback, not a forecast. Refuse to let circumstances control your mindset or actions.
- Focus on your vision, goals, and ability to create change from within rather than trusting circumstances. Circumstances bend to the will of those who refuse to accept them as final.
- Your future depends on your actions today, not on your past. Commit to making progress each day. Refuse to let the outside control the inside.
- Your goal should be your driving force, which you assume to be guaranteed. Discipline your thoughts and emotions

to align with your desired outcome, not your current circumstances.
- Results are feedback, not limitations. Sprint toward your results to understand what is going on inside you and make the necessary adjustments.
- Develop a world-class mindset by consciously choosing empowering thoughts and rejecting limiting ideas. Your subconscious will follow the programming you give it.
- Attitude is a game changer. Adopt a prosperous, positive mental attitude that looks for the good and assumes the feelings of already having what you want.

CHAPTER 11

Just Decide

I'll never forget the day I walked outside and saw the foreclosure sticker slapped on my garage. I had just lost my job. I was $150,000 in debt. Everything seemed to be falling apart. I remember standing there, staring at that sticker and realizing no one was coming to save me.

That was the moment I stopped negotiating with my circumstances. I didn't have a backup plan. I didn't have a plan B. I didn't have all the answers, but I had a choice and I made it. I decided that this wasn't how my story was going to end. I decided I was going to rise, not just survive, that I would rebuild my life, not with desperation, but with a real decision, the kind that changes everything. Here's what I've learned since then.

You don't need a perfect plan. You need a powerful decision. The moment you decide with finality, you gain access to a strength you didn't know you had. Doors open, and the right people show up. Life starts moving in your favor, not because of luck, but because you have finally moved in alignment with your purpose.

I remember the exact moment I truly decided. It was not when I said I wanted something or when I wrote it down, but when something clicked inside of me, like a flipped switch. I knew there was no turning back.

That's what this chapter is about. Real decisions are not made with logic alone. They're made with identity, with soul, with a fire in your gut, with a fire in your spirit that says, "I'm done waiting, I'm done doubting, I am creating the life that I'm proud of."

Transformation doesn't need time. It needs truth, and the truth is, you're one decision away from becoming unstoppable. So let's begin.

One idea changed my life: once I learned how important decisions were and I implemented this understanding with decision-making, my life changed. Decisions, or a lack of them, are responsible for making or breaking everything you desire in your life. People who become proficient at making decisions without being influenced by the opinions of others are the people whose annual incomes fall into the top income category. Napoleon Hill said decision is the starting point of achievement. In *Think and Grow Rich*, he reported that after interviewing 500 of the most successful people in the world, he found that their one common denominator was swift and effective decision-making.

In school, we're taught how to memorize, but we're not taught how to make decisions. You want to become a master at decision-making. I want you to have a PhD in it.

It isn't as if every decision you make is going to be a guaranteed win. But with the continual practice of making decisions that are greater than your current results, you're going to win over a three-month period. You're going to see how much these decisions are making or breaking you.

Get out of your head and get into your heart, which is where your power is. Stop overthinking, because that is the biggest saboteur. Why? Because it makes you hesitate: "I have to do this, then this, then this." No: just act. Take one action step. Think of a tree: if you were chopping down a tree, you wouldn't chop it down at one swing.

One Day or Day One?

Nothing happens until you make a decision and move. Every day, we're choosing either our old life or our world-class life. With our daily decisions, we're choosing either who we've been or who we're capable of being. It's either going to be one day or day one. You get to decide.

I want every reader of this book to know that every day is day one. I want you right now to think about what you want more than anything else in the world and how you really want to live. I want you to make an unshakable, irrevocable, committed decision. You create quantum leaps when you decide that comfort is not your standard. As long as you are loyal to comfort, quantum leaps are impossible. After you make a bold, all-in decision, with no plan B, your life will never be the same. The universe doesn't respond to indecision. It responds to bold, aligned, committed energy.

The first decision you have to make is to bet on yourself. Have the courage to go all-in on yourself. You have to want the transformation more than you want the comfort. People say that change takes time. That's the lie we've heard our whole lives. That's the lie we tell to protect ourselves.

Change requires decision. The greatest version of you appears when you stop negotiating with excuses. You have to take action that reflects your future, not your past. Your goals are great for your soul: we're goal seeking organisms. Your goal is not just a destination, it's your permission slip for becoming the person you're meant to be. Goals awaken your spirit. Targets give your soul something to aim for. Without a target, your power is scattered, but with a goal, you're focused, you're energized, you're dangerous in the best sense.

That's why goals matter so much—not just for achievement, but for aligning with your highest self. You must have a purpose. You must have a plan. You must take action, but the key is, you must be definite. Without definiteness, nothing changes.

Right now, think back to the goal that you want more than anything else. Build an enormous idea of yourself. See yourself as bigger, better, bolder than you've ever been. Every decision you make flows from the individual you believe you truly are; otherwise, nothing happens. There's no reason to make a decision unless you have an authentic want—a want that is yours—and you own your want. Your want is why you make the decision. You don't justify it to anybody.

But understand this: you have to want it as badly as you want to breathe. You must really want it. You do not have to know how you're going to get it, but you must want it in every cell of your being.

Write down exactly what you want more than anything else. From this point on, every decision is going to come from this want. Now your job is to believe in your goal—and in your ability to attain it—with every cell of your being, with unshakable confidence, unshakable certainty, and unshakable belief.

When you believe in the outcome before it's already happened, that's decision. You're planting seeds in your subconscious mind. Belief is knowing that you know. Belief is the catalyst that brings your goals to life. Belief activates certainty. Belief is the inner knowing that your goals are yours; they belong to you. This deep connection strengthens your commitments, eliminates self-doubt, and prevents you from giving up at the first sign of adversity. With belief, you train your mind to see possibilities rather than limitations.

Nothing is possible without a positive, prosperous mental attitude. I want to go deep into attitude because decision is an attitude. Attitude affects every aspect of your life. As you're reading these words, you have to realize that each word is an attitude. Now our attitude is the composite of our thoughts, our feelings, and our actions. Within each second, we have this power flowing through us. That's thought energy. We're accepting either a positive side of our personality or a negative side.

Whatever thought we accept with our imagination then travels out into the universe. But it also travels inside of us, inside our subconscious mind, and the universe boomerangs it back to us by the law of cause and effect. It will boomerang anything that is in harmony with the thought we have put out.

Our thoughts create our feelings, and our feelings are put out into the universe. The universe gives us exactly what's in harmony with the feelings that we feel, and then it puts our body into action. Our action creates the results. Attitude, then, is results.

> **Attitude: The Three-Step Process**
>
> 1. Thoughts   2. Feelings   3. Actions

Attitude is a three-step process: thoughts, feelings, actions. It's not just about being positive or optimistic; it's about alignment. When your mind is thinking the right thoughts, your heart is feeling the right emotions, and your body is taking the right actions, you are in harmony. That harmony creates results. It creates everything you experience.

When your attitude is off, it doesn't matter how hard you work or how smart you are: you're out of sync. But when your attitude is right, doors open, people respond differently, and success flows to you. I want your attitude to be such that as soon as you walk in a room, you're so comfortable with yourself that your vibration influences the room without your even saying a word. That is a positive, prosperous mental attitude.

You don't attract what you want; you attract what you *are*. That's why changing your attitude changes your results. It changes your vibration. Everything in life responds to vibration. You're either drawing success in or pushing it away based on the frequency you're on. Attitude is more important than talent, more important than education, because it's the foundation of how you show up, how you think, how you speak, and how you act.

So if there's one thing to master, master your attitude. Your attitude expresses your thoughts, feelings, and actions. When all three are aligned, you become unstoppable. Your attitude is a thermostat of your life. It determines how high you rise or how low you stay.

Attitude is more than mere positivity. It's the lens through which you see the world and the energy you bring to every experience. Your attitude shapes your expectations, and your expectations shape your outcome. Attitude is your silent influencer. It speaks louder than words and shapes how others respond to you even before you speak. It's your competitive advantage.

Attitude is your silent influencer.

    Life doesn't always go our way, but attitude determines whether you shrink or stretch in adversity. You don't control circumstances, but you always control your responses, and the response is where your power lies. Success is an inside-outside game. A winning attitude aligns your mind with possibility, your actions with purpose, and your outcomes with excellence. Energy flows where attitude goes. When your attitude is right, effort feels lighter, ideas flow faster, and people are drawn to your presence.

    Years ago, I called Bob Proctor and said, "Bob, I'm really stuck."

"Why are you stuck?"

"Because I'm letting the results control me."

"Arash, you know better. That's a dumb idea. If you get what I'm about to tell you, everything's going to change. I learned this from one of my mentors, and I want you to learn this right now. Anybody can have a great attitude when things are going well," he said, "but the true pros in life have an even better attitude when things are not going as well."

    He told me to stop living my life as an amateur and start being a pro.

    Something inside of me woke up that day. There was a giant inside of me that experienced a huge aha! I've never been the same since. I spent two years studying my attitude. I would observe what would trigger a bad attitude.

    One day I had a leak in my roof, and I started laughing. I was laughing because I had been in such a negative attitude the day before. I told myself that I deserved this attitude.

    When you understand that it's not about perfection, it's about consistency, your life will change. You can't always control what happens, but you can always control the meaning you give to it, and your meaning creates your momentum.

Attitude creates our results, thoughts, feelings, and actions. Decide today to stop waiting for outside circumstances to change, and start changing yourself from the inside out. You must live now like the you who already have what you want. That's decision. Walk like it, talk like it, act like it, dress like it, think like it, serve like it. This is how you are in absolute alignment with your magnificent future.

Ideas without action aren't ideas. They're regrets. Your mind doesn't care what you plant in it. It is your responsibility to guard your mind. If your emotions are stronger than your mindset, you will make decisions based on your present results—from what the outside is showing you.

There is a difference between wishing for a thing and being ready to receive it. No one is ready for a thing until they believe they can acquire it. The state of mind must be belief, not mere hope or wish.

Consider what Napoleon Hill said: "Open-mindedness is a crucial factor in forming and maintaining beliefs." Let's dissect this quote.

Open-mindedness is essential for belief. I work with clients all over the world, and when they're stuck, I always refer back to this quote, and I'll ask them this one question: are you ready to receive what you want?

They often respond, "I am absolutely ready to receive it."

Then I ask them, "Can you tell me what you did for the last few days? What were your thoughts? What types of actions did you take?"

"I did what I normally do."

"Then you're not ready to receive it. You're never going to be ready for a thing until you are willing to behave before you're even ready. We have to behave our way into a new identity. We have to be willing to fail rather than succeeding at our present selves. If your belief is that you will do it *someday*, that's not a decision; that's procrastination. If your belief is, 'I'm not good enough,' you will sabotage every blessing and opportunity that shows up in your life."

I want you to make an elimination list of the beliefs that are sabotaging you, and I want you to cut the cord. Let them go, and really think from your goal. Which beliefs are not in harmony with that goal? Which beliefs are not in harmony with your future self or with the person who's already achieved what you most want to achieve?

Make a list of these obstructive beliefs, then just let them go. Once you write the list, you're taking these beliefs out of your energy.

Keep going. It's a daily commitment to becoming your best self and achieving your goal. Keep pivoting forward, and understand that beliefs are created from past experiences. Behaviors that are incongruent with ourselves won't last, so we can't make decisions for only three days a week. We have to decide and form the habit of following through on that decision all day, every day.

Reprogramming your mind is about daily intention. It's about intentional repetition, daily acceptance, and rejecting thoughts from the point of view of your goal and future self.

Every time you think a thought, you are wiring your brain.

I cannot share this idea enough. I have brought it up multiple times throughout this book for a reason: this is how you rewire your mind for success. Every time you think a thought, you are rewiring your brain. The more you repeat similar thoughts, the easier it becomes to think that way again and again, and it will become automatic.

I want you to embrace this philosophy of intentional repetition. Repetition has no power if it is just a matter of checking a box with no emotion or intention. But when you link intentional repetition with knowingness, with the decision that the outcome is already done, you're going to rewire yourself for the life you really want. Intentional repetition transforms your thinking. When you transform your thinking, you transform your beliefs, and when you transform your beliefs, you transform your results. If you begin to think thoughts of abundance, you will build new highways in your mind that will lead you to freedom.

This is why autosuggestion matters. This is why visualization matters. This is why your declarations and self-talk matter, and this is why your decisions matter. You are reprogramming the deepest layers of your identity.

But as I've already emphasized, in order to become what you want, you must overcome the old you, and the side effect is discomfort. Discomfort is a great state. Keep doing what you're uncomfortable with. That's when decision comes to your aid. Just decide every day that you're going to get 1 percent better at becoming the best version of yourself.

Think about your current results: this is where you are right now. Then think of your goal. Your job is to know where you are and where you want to go. All you have to do is fill in that gap. That gap is always the decision made by the person you're going to become. That is the identity gap. Procrastination is the bad habit of putting off until the day after tomorrow what should have been done the day before yesterday. *Do it now* is a decision. *Do it now* is the greatest brain tattoo that I've ever shared with clients. It will create results literally overnight.

Every action we take has a purpose. I want you to be purposeful. If you're not operating purposefully, you're not operating from a decision. We cannot talk about decision without action. There is no decision if it's not followed through with action; it's delusion.

But I don't want you to take just any type of action: I want it to be inspired. Inspiration means *spirit*. I want you to be completely detached from the outcome. I want you to be free. I want you to be loose. We want to make a move before we're ready, but action is the bridge between intention and thoughts. It is not enough to think wealthy thoughts, speak wealthy words, and envision a big future. Action is the physical proof that you truly believe what you say you believe. Without bold action, you are just wishing and hoping, and wishing and hoping have no power.

Action is spirit-led. It's powerful. It's done with great strategy. Bold action separates the takers from the leaders. Many people stay stuck not because they lack opportunities, but because they hesitate, they doubt, and they overthink. Wealth always responds to those who move before they're ready. Bold action means you are committed to doing the work, whether or not you see instant results.

> We are rewarded in public
> for what we do in private.

What you do daily when no one is watching will determine whether you rise to your next level of freedom. We are rewarded in public for what we do in private. Bold action requires you to leave your comfort zone. You cannot grow inside your comfort zone. You must be willing to do uncomfortable things in a great way. You must make uncomfortable investments to get to your next level of freedom.

When you hesitate, you lose opportunity, you lose momentum, and you align with suffering rather than with the freedom you desire. Over the last twenty years, I've come to realize that when you act on ideas right away, you're giving yourself a shot to win big.

Let's close this chapter by making sure we really understand decisions. Understand that every thought, every feeling, and every action is a frequency. Frequencies are levels of vibration. We think on frequencies, so we attract on frequencies. Your current results are the consequences of the thoughts and the frequency that you have been thinking on. You have a goal on a much higher frequency. In order to get from where you are to where you want to go, the first thing you have to do is make that unshakable, irrevocable, nonnegotiable decision: "This is what I'm creating, no matter what."

> When you make the decision,
> the way shows itself.

When you make the decision, the way shows itself. If you make the decision one day but don't follow through on it day in and day out, you will keep creating the same thoughts, feelings, and actions that will duplicate your current results. You will attract the same environment over and over again, and the goal will slip away. The goal then turns into a mere repetition of what you have now.

But when you make an irrevocable, committed decision, your mind jumps onto the frequency of your goal. Your job is to stay on that frequency. Once it is an unshakable decision, repeated day in and day out, regardless of appearances, you will start thinking and acting like the person you want to become.

Decision is the chief principle that has activated my life. My decision was saying no to comfort and a guaranteed job. I followed it up with doing uncomfortable things day in and day out.

I want you to act now. There's never any time but now, and there will never be any time but now. Do everything with enthusiasm, do it with a purpose, but do it now.

Decision will change your life. I know it's changed mine, and it's changed the lives of millions of people. Without it, your goals and wants are only a delusion. Delusion will keep you repeating the same thoughts, feelings, actions, results, and relationships, but decision opens the door to a life of freedom.

Emerson said that once you make a decision, the whole universe conspires on your behalf to make it a reality. Decide now.

Key Points in This Chapter

- To transform your life and achieve your goals, make clear, irrevocable decisions. Change doesn't require time, but it does require a committed decision.
- The universe responds to bold, aligned decisions, not to indecision or negotiation. Make a decision to rise, not just survive. This is the first step to accessing inner strength and moving your life in a positive direction.
- Consider the role of attitude, belief, and intentional repetition in reprogramming your mindset and behaviors. Eliminate limiting beliefs. Live as the person who has already achieved your desired outcome.

- After making a decision, take immediate, inspired action rather than hesitating or overthinking. Wealth and success respond to those who move forward even when they don't feel fully ready.
- Once an irrevocable decision is made, the entire universe will conspire to make it a reality. The key is committing fully to the decision rather than wavering or making decisions from your current circumstances.

CHAPTER 12

The Role of Environment in Your Transformation

You don't rise to the level of your intentions. You fall to the level of your environment. No matter how strong your willpower or how clear your goals, if your environment is working against you, success becomes a daily uphill battle.

Your environment is always influencing you, shaping your habits, your standards, your energy, and your expectations. Most people try to change their lives without changing their environment, and they wonder why nothing sticks. Think about this: Would you try to stay sober if you went to a bar every day? Would you try to lose weight working in a bakery?

Yet every day, people attempt to transform their lives while staying trapped in environments that reinforce the old version of themselves. When you upgrade your environment, transformation becomes automatic. You don't have to fight the old. You simply step into a space that makes the new version of you inevitable.

In this chapter, I'll show you how to engineer environments that pull you toward success, elevate your identity, and make the old version of you obsolete.

When my life changed, my environment changed. Throughout this book, I've shared many stories of the deep impact my mentor had on me. One of the first lessons I learned was that I had to upgrade my environment. The people I surrounded myself with represented the exact life I was going to create. Your environment is either setting you up to win or holding you back.

Most people stay stuck because they're loyal to old environments. They fear letting go of the old even when it no longer serves them. They are afraid of hurting other people's feelings, and they take comfort in the familiar.

When you grow, you will start attracting people at much higher levels of thinking, standards, and goals. I got an email from an old client who said, "Arash, I haven't spoken with you in two years, but you changed my life." I had shared one insight about environment that changed the game for this gentleman. He said, "You told me, 'Show me your circle, I'll show you your future.' From that moment, I changed my circle, and over the last two years, I've had the best two years of my life."

The same was true for me. I upgraded my environment and learned how to create ideas from people who were implementing bigger ideas. I would study them like a scientist. I would watch how they walked. I would watch how they dressed. I would study their standards. One thing that was very common: they were the most disciplined people I had ever been around.

Here's a suggestion: Reach out to somebody that you admire, someone that has already created something like the life you want. Call them and invite them to coffee. If they're not in the same town, ask them if they'll get on a call with you. Pick their brain, and be transparent about it. Just by doing that, you will change the game. You'll be quite surprised at their willingness to have a conversation with you.

Never shrink to fit in.

Understand that success, like environment, leaves clues: this will set you up for massive transformation. Show me the five people you talk to the most, and I'll show you your results. Your thinking is always mirrored by your circle.

Have you outgrown your circle? Is it time to attract a higher standard? Never shrink to fit in. Conforming chips away at your self-esteem.

Proximity also shapes your belief system and behavior. Proximity has to do with the people around whom you consistently spend your time. Your circle reflects your standards, your growth, and your results.

Do an energy audit. Ask yourself if the people in your closest circle today energize you or drain you. If they energize you, stay around them. If they drain you, minimize your time with them. You don't need to cut people off. Simply shift your energy toward surrounding yourself with more connections that are aligned with your goals. Anyone who drains your energy is also affecting your attitude.

I'm not saying that you have to limit your acquaintance to people who are extremely successful: there could be somebody that you just love being around and have a lot of fun with. I'm not telling you to remove those people. But don't spend time with anybody that sucks your energy. Don't spend time with somebody that complains, don't spend time with negativity, because it will eventually become part of you. We become like those we hang around with. If you look at a given group of people from a health standpoint, you'll probably find that they're very similar. The same is likely to be true from a wealth standpoint.

Beware of low standards. Your environment sets your standard. If you are in an environment that is satisfied with a six-figure income but you want to create a seven- and eight-figure business, you have to set yourself up in the environment of seven- and eight-figure thinkers. You will raise your standards from the first moment that you're in that environment.

Be careful about your sources of advice. Don't take advice from someone living a life you wouldn't want to live. Would you want to live the life of the person who is advising you? Are you getting input from people who have created the results you want? That will tell you the story.

Physical space equals mental clarity. A tidy space equals a productive mind. Clutter creates chaos. Order is heaven's first law. If your space is messy, your mind sees only chaos. When you're in chaos, you're set up to lose. If you have chaos, your mind is in chaos.

The same is true with your digital environment. I joke with certain friends: "You have 30,000 unread emails. You're never going to read them. Get rid of them, because all your mind is seeing is chaos."

The more successful you become, the smaller and more intentional your circle will be. You want to become superintentional about those who are mentoring you. Smaller circle, stronger values. Less is more. You want to be in an environment where there are no excuses, no complaining, no low goals, and no low effort. You want to be in an environment with high goals and high achievers. You value your environment so much that you loathe negativity.

Upgrade through proximity. High-level thinkers stretch your identity. They choose challenge over comfort. They stretch beyond comfort zones to gain access to new levels of massive quantum leaps.

Upgrade through proximity.

Even when I was thinking I was limited, I always surrounded myself with people who were more aware than I was. Their awareness affected me in an extremely positive way. The people you surround yourself with are either empowering you or impairing you. Raise the bar. Form support groups. Initiate growth conversation. Join study groups. Go to seminars; hire mentors.

Immersive experiences accelerate growth. You can always measure the investment in time and money, but you can never measure where it'll take you. Conversely, maybe you will be the catalyst who wakes up your environment and raises the standards of those around you. Proximity is power.

Key Points in This Chapter

- Your environment is critical in shaping your transformation and personal growth.
- Your environment strongly influences your habits, standards, energy, and expectations. Trying to change without changing your environment is an uphill battle.
- Upgrading your environment makes transformation automatic. You don't have to fight the old; you simply step into a new space that supports the new version of you.
- The people you surround yourself with reflect the life you will create. Associating with higher-level thinkers and achievers can elevate your own standards and results.
- A tidy, organized physical environment promotes mental clarity and productivity. Clear away clutter and chaos.
- As you become more successful, being intentional about your inner circle becomes crucial. Surround yourself with those who share your values and push you to grow.

CHAPTER 13

Mentorship: The Shortcut to Success

Success leaves clues, but most people are too busy guessing, struggling, or trying to figure it out on their own to notice them. The fastest path to success is not through trial and error but through mentorship.

You can take the long road filled with dead ends, mistakes, and unnecessary setbacks, or you can model yourself on someone who's already been where you want to go. Mentorship compresses decades into days. Most people wear a self-made badge of honor, but it's actually a badge of struggle. Doing it alone might feel noble, but it's expensive in time, energy, money, and missed opportunities.

When you have the right mentor, you borrow their belief, their standards, their experience, their wisdom, and their mistakes without paying the same price. You go step by step, shoulder by shoulder, with them, and you see further, faster, bigger results and achieve more with less resistance.

In this chapter, I'm going to show you why mentorship isn't optional for the serious achiever: it's essential. I will also show you how to attract the right mentors, maximize those relationships, and become the kind of person mentors want to foster.

In our first conversation, my mentor, Bob Proctor, said, "Arash, I want you to do exactly what I tell you to do. Don't do half; don't do three fourths."

At this time, I didn't have a job, I was $150,000 in debt, and I was struggling. I was getting married in three weeks.

When I committed to being mentored by Bob, our agreement was that I was going to do exactly what he told me to do without question. He used to tell me, "I'm not going to tell you what time to wake up, but I'm going to show you exactly what to do. Your job is to follow the directions."

"Arash," he told me, "the only thing people are missing is direction."

Soon after we started our mentorship, I got a call from Bob, and he said, "I want you to jump on a flight to come see me in Toronto." He wanted me to come the very next day. All I was thinking was how much money the flight was going to cost, because I didn't have any money, but I had committed to doing exactly what he told me.

The only thing people are missing is direction.

This flight changed my life. When I was sitting on the plane, I was wondering what I was doing: I was being reckless. But I followed through, because I had told myself I was going to do exactly what Bob told me for a year and see if mentorship really works.

I landed in Toronto. Bob's grandson Danny picked me up and took me to Bob's house. Bob said, "Arash, you came."

"I know. I told you I was going to do exactly what you told me to do."

"I was testing you to see how serious you were."

"This was a test?"

"Don't worry; I'm going to make it worthwhile."

That night he took me out to one of his favorite steak houses, and for three hours we discussed so many ideas that I was never the same afterward. That trip changed my belief in mentorship, not because my results changed that night, but I had a crystal clear picture of where he was taking me, and I believed in what he was doing.

The old me would never have gotten on that plane. I would have made many excuses. I've said that it is essential to behave your way into a new identity, and that is exactly what I did that day. Right away when I got home, I implemented the first few ideas that Bob suggested, and they changed my results.

The ultimate cheat code is mentorship.

The ultimate cheat code is mentorship. Following what a mentor tells you to do will minimize the time to success. You will reduce the time and mistakes just by following their direction.

What Is Mentorship?

A mentor is someone who sees your potential and holds the image of who you can be before you see it. A mentor will eliminate your blind spots, speak the truth to you, and show you a proven path forward. A mentor speeds up growth and collapses time. They instill belief and clarity, and they make it so simple. They provide direction, accountability, and mindset.

My turning point was the flight that changed my life. I hope this book is your turning point. One decision changed my life within thirty days. At the time, I didn't know it would do that, but those thirty days turned into another thirty days and another thirty days. Now, eighteen years later, I've never turned back.

"Bob," I said when I began, "I've been studying this work for three years."

"You don't know it. You know *about* it. Just look at your results. The results always tell you how well you understand what you're studying. Information without implementation is delusion. Success never comes from doing it itself. Nor does it come from doing more, but from doing the right things consistently, compounded over time."

A great mentor won't tell you what you *want* to hear, but what you *need* to hear. A great mentor will be counterintuitive to your belief system; otherwise, you would already be doing what you need to do, and you would already be achieving the results.

In my first year of mentorship, I committed to one year with no fallback. I was all-in. That commitment allowed me to implement the framework and processes my mentor had given to me. Over the next twelve months, I committed to delayed gratification; I turned growth into a game. That's when everything changed.

A great mentor will get you to choose action over fear. You can never think your way out of fear. You act your way out of it.

One day Bob was sharing a story about W. Clement Stone, the great businessman and self-help author. "Arash," he said, "I implemented this when I learned this from Clement Stone, which was, *do it now*."

That was one of the first things that I did within the first thirty days. I made doing it now not just my standard, not just a philosophy, but my identity. I stopped waiting for the perfect time. The true cost of waiting is millions of dollars in opportunities.

The true cost of waiting is millions of dollars in opportunities.

Most people delay action until they feel ready. They're always planning to plan. The real cost is in time, confidence, and unrealized potential. Mentorship is not advice; it's direction. It's transformation through accountability, belief, and repetition. Mentors don't teach you *what* to think. They teach you *how* to think.

One day my mentor drew a target: circles inside of circles inside of circles. He said, "This is the mistake most people make—why they don't create results. They'll study my work and then a couple months later, they'll study Tony Robbins's work. A couple months later, they'll study Jack Canfield's work. They never go to the bull's-eye.

"I want you to pick one mentor, do exactly what they tell you to do, and focus only on that mentor's philosophy. This will allow you to go very deep, and your reward is going to be your results. Depth is always greater than quantity. Surface-level advice equals surface-level results. You want to find a mentor who has already achieved the results that you want to achieve. They already have proven results personally.

"A great mentor is very honest and operates with high standards that will become your standards. Your future then is a done deal. They never mentor you from your current self. They always are mentoring you from who you can be. Your job is to be coachable beyond comfort."

Ten years later, I called Bob and said, "I figured out the trick to mentorship. I know why I really changed."

"What do you think it is?"

"Before, I was gathering information, and I would always do what the mentors gave me to do that were comfortable for me. When I worked with you, I did whatever you told me regardless of comfort or discomfort. The key to mentorship is to do exactly what the mentor tells you, not just what you're comfortable with. You follow direction even when it's uncomfortable. Let go of your ego and old patterns."

Follow direction even when it's uncomfortable.

Here's a common misconception: People don't want to pay the price for mentorship. But they pay a lot more in time, mistakes, and investments than it would cost for a great mentor. Some say they can figure it out on their own. That's too expensive. I used to think that way, but that's the biggest misconception. You're going to spend the time and money anyway on whatever you're spending it on.

One idea can transform your life by millions. A lot of people say they are not ready yet, but you're never going to be ready for a thing until you do it. Emerson said, "Do the thing and you shall have the power, but they who do not do the thing have not the power." He doesn't say to get *ready* for the thing: *doing* the thing will give you power.

Mentorship is an investment, not a cost. I've invested millions of dollars in mentorship over the past twenty years, but I changed my philosophy around it, because I've gotten really good at executing ideas. If I invested $50,000, I would turn that into several hundred thousand dollars by executing the ideas. One idea can take you far if you shift your mindset from cost to value.

The right mentor will save you years of trial and error. You can always measure the cost, but you can never measure where the work will take you. Ask yourself who is currently guiding you and whether you are being stretched. Are you being held accountable? Are you getting proper direction? What is the cost of staying where you are? Everything is a cost. Time is our greatest currency. The last question is, are you truly creating the life you want?

When you ask these questions, you may want to find a mentor who can show you the way. Watch how magical your life will become. Mentorship is the greatest cheat code.

Key Points in This Chapter

- Mentorship can be a shortcut to success.
- Mentorship enables you to borrow the experience, wisdom, and beliefs of someone who has already achieved the results you want without having to pay the same price.
- A good mentor will eliminate your blind spots, speak the truth, and show you a proven path forward, accelerating your growth and success.
- To get the most out of mentorship, you must be willing to do exactly what the mentor tells you to do, even if it's outside your comfort zone.
- Mentorship is an investment, not a cost. The right mentor can save you years of trial and error and help you achieve results far beyond what you could on your own.

CHAPTER 14

The Power of Process

High performers don't rely on willpower. They rely on systems, processes, and frameworks. They don't leave success to chance. They build it into their day, their habits, and their environment through intentional checklists, processes, and rituals.

Most people think success requires constant motivation, but motivation fades. What creates consistent, unstoppable progress is habits and routines that remove thinking, eliminate friction, and lead to excellence. When you see someone succeeding at a high level, you're really seeing a system at work behind the scenes. This invisible checklist ensures the win before the day even begins. Habits and routines act as your autopilot for success. They free up mental energy, create predictable momentum, and make high performance feel automatic, even on your worst days.

In this chapter, I'll show you how to create your own high-performance checklist, rituals, and routines that lock in your standards, minimize distractions, and make success inevitable.

Your processes create results by default. The processes you implement at the starting point create massive transformation, because transformation happens as a result of your processes.

Build a new model that makes the old model obsolete. It is much easier to create a new model than to change the old one. Yet most people are constantly trying to change the old and then build the new. It will never happen.

> It is much easier to create a new model than to change the old one.

For the first process, I want you to build a big idea of yourself every single day. How do you do that? In your morning routine, you write out your perfect day every morning. When you write out your perfect day in the present tense with emotional words, you are planting those ideas in your subconscious mind. Writing creates feelings, feelings create actions, and actions create results. Writing is particularly advantageous because it deepens your commitment on a subconscious level.

The Millionaire Morning Routine

The process of creating a morning routine changes the game. Years ago, I developed my millionaire morning routine, which has been a game changer in my life and for thousands of other people.

Once you wake up, set up your morning routine and write out your goal. You're training yourself to come from your goal. Then think about ten things that you're grateful for, but don't make this a merely intellectual exercise. You want to get in the vibration of gratitude, because gratitude activates abundance in your life. So think about ten things you're grateful for and then ask yourself why you are grateful. If you're grateful for your dogs, name your dogs and say why. For your kids? For your experiences?

Write out twenty "I am" statements. "I am" is declaring who you are. This is an identity changer. *I am powerful. I am wealthy, I am successful. I am healthy.* When you write out "I am" statements every day, you're reshaping your identity.

Meditate. If you don't regularly meditate, start with ten minutes a day of just quieting your mind. Journal, write out your goal, and write out only ideas of how you can achieve your goal. With this morning ritual of journaling, you are creating a prosperity consciousness. Autosuggestion is a suggestion from yourself to yourself: *I am so happy and grateful now that I am earning $100,000 or more every month, and I love it.* With repeated autosuggestion day in and day out, you are rewiring your new program.

Read books: read fifteen minutes a day in the morning, and exercise.

This powerful morning ritual will change your confidence. It's telling the world that your goals mean something to you, and it's telling your subconscious mind that you value yourself.

Mentally rehearse visualizing every day. It's a great process to make into a habit. Your imagination takes you everywhere. Now go on and operate your day.

Activating the Dog

In my company, we say that there is a dog inside of you that's dying to come out. What is a dog? It's an individual who operates with grit, courage, perseverance, and passion. It's somebody who is extremely confident and secure. They're not passive. They're active. They're creating their lives. They're never worried about what other people think of them, because their inner essence is obsessed with their goal, with impacting other people, and with their ideas.

A dog's instinct drives them. They're on an instinctive path while blazing their own trail; they're never overthinking. Dogs are humble and hungry for growth. They want to be more, have more, and do more, and they are obsessed with continually improving. Their personal development is sacred.

You may be playing your life as a watcher: overthinking, hiding, worried about what people think. How you can activate that dog inside you? I'm going to give you the exact process that has launched many people into their alternate identity. That's the real you.

Dogs develop an attitude through passion. They let their passion drive them. That passion will move everything in your favor. You think and act from your alternate identity. You never hesitate, you never judge. You never worry about failure. Dogs create momentum with attacking action. They act with unwavering confidence. Dogs bring definiteness into each hour. They have made a committed, irrevocable decision: "I'm doing this no matter what." They constantly activate their fearlessness.

Everything you are driven by, in every process, always goes back to how we started this book: what do you really want more than anything else? You radically accept only what you want. When you do this, you're putting your want on steroids, and it will turn into a desire. You never worry about the how. You never worry about the circumstances.

By radically accepting your idea, you are making your future a magnificent obsession. You are building your vision and making it stronger and stronger every day. Focusing on your vision is the driving force in your life. Goals are your vision of the future. Fall in love with your future. Design your life masterpiece.

Most people have fears of the future. If you do, you'll be shrinking all the time. You will be losing out on opportunity after opportunity. Once you've made that irrevocable commitment, I want you to count on your ability to design a world-class future.

Count on your ability to design a world-class future.

Now that you know what you want, it's time to believe it with every cell of your being. With unshakable belief—when you believe in the outcome before it's happening—you are planting seeds in your subconscious mind, and as we have seen, whatever you plant in your subconscious will grow. Belief is knowing. Now that we have desire, we turn the want into knowing.

Belief is the catalyst that brings your goals to life. Belief activates certainty; it is the inner knowing that your goals belong to you. This deep connection strengthens your commitment, eliminates self-doubts, and prevents you from giving up at the first sign of adversity. With belief, you train your mind to see possibilities rather than limitations.

Belief creates urgency, but beliefs are created from past experience. The practice of autosuggestion and visualization, mental rehearsal every day, will rebuild your beliefs. Most people are working from an outdated belief about the past, but when you follow the future self framework, you are installing new beliefs.

The future self framework is a powerful process that I've discussed throughout this book. I am repeating it because of how powerfully it will transform your life. From this moment forward, you commit to this framework of your future self, and you make every decision from the goal already achieved. You operate every attitude as the person who has the most prosperous and positive mental attitude. You build every standard as the person who's already achieved your goal. You think, feel, act, and transform your identity as the person who has achieved that goal, and you build one discipline at a time. You focus on your pinnacle discipline, which will raise the level of all your other disciplines. Action is the key, but when you take action, take inspired action. Take it with confidence. Bring it in with your alternate identity, and be detached from the outcome.

I want you to practice making your hours epic. You're going to focus on your thirty-, sixty-, and ninety-minute sprints, and you are going to commit to a minimum of three goal-achieving activities from the goal already achieved, as well as the three wins. It is always the quality of the work, not the quantity, that matters. The three goal-achieving activities stacked will create massive results.

Five great hours a day create a world-class life. The more discipline you have, the more confidence you have. The results always come from practicing your processes consistently over time.

Five great hours a day create a world-class life.

Let's work on philosophy. Nothing owns you. Stepping away and being detached from the outcome is stepping away from fear. A change of feeling is always a change of destiny. Train your emotional state to feel as you would feel had you already achieved your goal. You would feel pride; I want you to feel proud now. You'd feel excited; I want you to feel excited. You'd have peace of mind; I want you to feel how it feels when you are emotionally free. Ask yourself every day what it feels like now that you are prosperous.

When you start feeling free, your game changes, and life becomes magical. You train yourself to detach from your five senses and discipline them to see what you will see when you achieve your goal—to hear people congratulating you, to smell a celebration dinner. Discipline your five senses rather than letting them discipline you. When you go to the unknown, which is beyond your comfort zone and your senses, you create freedom.

Most people create from a place of lack and limitation. Create from a place of wholeness, from worthiness. Worthiness is your divine right. Declare that you are worthy and deserving of the good that you desire.

When you get to the point where you have what you desire, the universe will realize that you're out of the way. Now all the good that you desire is drawn to you effortlessly. It's always about allowing. If we're attached to anything, it owns us.

The Winning Process

Stay loose and stay free, but the winning process that I'm going to give you right now will change the game. I've changed many people's lives with it. It starts with what you really want. The want will inspire you to make an irrevocable, committed decision. Your goal requires you to have courage, but the decision will activate more courage in you. The courage in turn will activate confidence. Every goal you have demands that you raise your confidence. The confidence in turn will activate discipline. The discipline activates action, and the action will create the results. This is the winning process.

When you practice this process, you change the game. I advise you to prioritize the process that will create the greatest impact when you start. I recommend starting with the millionaire morning process described above. Practice that every day.

The Winning Process

1. Start with what you really want.
2. The want inspires you to make an irrevocable, committed decision.
3. The decision activates courage in you.
4. The courage activates confidence.
5. The confidence activates discipline.
6. The discipline activates action.
7. The action creates the results.

Once you've create the habit of the millionaire mornings, add the next process as your goal demands. Your processes create your results. But you don't have to carry out all the processes in this book. Start by installing the most important process that your vision, your goal, and your standards demand.

Key Points in This Chapter

- Strategies for achieving high performance and success include building a morning routine focused on visualizing your goals, practicing gratitude, and positive affirmations.
- Develop an alternate identity, or "dog mindset," that is driven by passion, confidence, and an unwavering commitment to your goals.
- Use the future self framework: make decisions and act from the perspective of one who has already achieved your goals.
- Practice detachment from outcomes. Focus on the process and quality of your work rather than on external results.
- To build momentum and confidence, start by implementing the most powerful processes, such as the millionaire mornings routine.

CHAPTER 15

Commit First, Solve Later: Trust the Process

The world as you see it is only a reflection of what you believe. When the way seems clear, it is because your mind is focused on the solution, not the problem. What you hold in your imagination with unwavering faith must manifest in external results.

What are you holding in your imagination? Are you holding what you want or what you don't want? Are you reading these words right now without explicit trust in yourself? Are you trusting the process? Are you practicing the processes? Are you implementing the ideas that will allow you to soar or the ones that are merely allowing you to gather information?

In self-help, there are two camps. One type is constantly reading book after book and listening to YouTube after YouTube. Then there's the camp that is committed to transformation—that understands.

Trust is critical to your success. Every thought and every image you hold is an invitation to the universe to bring forth great results. Do not let the outside world deceive you. What you see now is temporary. It has only been created by your past thinking, feelings, actions, and identity. Trust is the catalyst for transformation. Once you place trust in the process, you will see the way open up for you.

When you are in worry, doubt, and fear, immediately shift to trust. Your results merely reflect the thoughts and beliefs of which you are the most convinced in your heart. You are only controlled by circumstances if you allow that. Whenever we allow circumstances to control us, we're not thinking; we're not operating from our future self. We're not making decisions from the goal already achieved.

Every obstacle and every challenge you face is an opportunity to build more trust in yourself. Your mind is shaping and molding everything you experience. Who controls your mind? Do you, or are you the victim of your mind? As we've seen, discipline is critical for controlling and shaping your mind to create the life you want.

Who controls your mind?

When you trust God to make a way out of your circumstances, you are aligning yourself with the incredible forces of the universe. There is no limitation to your faith. If you can imagine it, you can experience it. The difficulty is always lack of belief. Doubt and hesitation block the flow of the solution you seek. Whenever you have a doubt, I want you to train yourself to say, "That was the old me." When you acknowledge the old you and you reaffirm your goal, you've already achieved it. You have rewired your mind.

You must let go of fear and uncertainty. Fear is designed to help you, not stop you. Every time you fear taking some action, you must take it right away. When you trust, the way becomes clear. The universe will always work out all the details when you are out of the way and let go of the need to control them. When you focus on the solution, you see all the possibilities. We are always the only problem we're ever going to have, as well as the only solution. When you focus only on what you really want, the way will show itself.

Power and trust do not lie in the belief that the way will be easy or that you will never face challenges. Yet no matter what adversity comes your way, you have the ability to ascend and rise above it. Challenges are not obstacles: they're stepping stones for greater things.

Trust is crucial for creating transformation and freedom. Trust cannot be forced. It's not a mental exercise: it's a state of being; it's just who you are. Trust that every step you take is unfolding for your highest and best good. The universe is always conspiring to bring everything you need, but it requires your full trust to reveal the way. It requires you to detach yourself completely from the outcome.

When you trust, you open yourself up to infinite possibilities. Right now, there are millions of ways to get to your goal. The universe is much wiser than we are. Trust the universe to work in your favor. The energy of trust aligns you with the flow of abundance, whereby all things you desire come into your life. It will happen automatically. Every day, people create success automatically, just as every day, there are people who fail. Align yourself with the behaviors of a person who succeeds automatically.

Trust the universe to work in your favor.

Trust is another word for *expectation*. Trust allows you to release worry, doubt, and fear effortlessly and opens the door to abundance. When you surrender the need to control, you align yourself with the flow of the universe, and life becomes magical. Your worthiness elevates and transforms you. You are never a victim of your circumstances. Change your beliefs, and the world around you must change. This change always begins with trust. Without it there is no faith, and there can be no significant results.

When you trust the universe, you trust that the universe aligns itself with all you desire. When you doubt, you're pushing all the good away from you.

The power of trust lies in delayed gratification. It is another one of your competitive advantages, because the majority of people do not understand delayed gratification. They start, stop, start, stop.

Every challenge you face is an opportunity to strengthen your trust. Your strength always comes out when you have a big purpose and you understand that you are absolutely amazing. You deserve a lot more than you are even going after.

The universe is always working on your behalf. Your job is to decide, think, feel, act, and get out of the way. Now the universe can work with you, because you are out of the way.

It is not your effort that determines your outcome, but your trust. Although everyone wants evidence before they trust, creation always begins with trust, not evidence. When you trust, you're aligning your emotions with the infinite potential of the universe. You are telling the universe, "I am ready to receive the good that I desire, and I'm grateful for the blessings that are already in motion." That's true faith and true trust in action.

Like everything else, trust must be cultivated consistently . It's not what you do once in a while; it's what you do every day that creates a world-class life. It is a state of being.

The power of trust lies in releasing yourself from the struggle and allowing your dreams to happen effortlessly. The way is being made even when you cannot see it. Build your trust as an identity-based behavior: trust is a characteristic that you are going to leverage to ascend, transform, and create a life of freedom for you, your family, and everyone around you.

Key Points in This Chapter

- The power of trust is crucial for achieving transformation and creating the life you desire.
- Trust is the catalyst for transformation. When you place trust in the process, the way will open up for you.
- Your thoughts and beliefs shape your reality. Focus on what you want rather than what you don't want.
- Challenges are opportunities to build more trust in yourself and rise above adversity.
- Trust aligns you with the flow of abundance in the universe and allows you to release worry, doubt, and fear.

- Trust is a state of being, not just a mental exercise, and it must be cultivated consistently.
- When you trust the universe, it conspires to bring you what you desire, but you must get out of the way and let it work.

A Final Word: Step Into the Goal Achieved

This book has been all about the transformative power of self-identity, personal development, and discipline. My story of transitioning from this situation to becoming a successful multimillion-dollar business owner and influential coach is a testament to the principles discussed in this book. I hope that sharing my journey will give you inspiration and practical steps for embarking on your path to success and fulfillment.

About twenty years ago, my life was far from the success and fulfillment I experience today. I was deeply entrenched in the corporate world, earning a low six-figure income, yet still finding myself $150,000 in debt. Despite the outward appearance of success, my life was not fulfilling, and I realized something fundamentally needed to change. My journey into personal development began with the book *Think and Grow Rich* by Napoleon Hill. Back then, finding guidance was a struggle, unlike today, when there is easy access to mentors and resources. I spent years attending seminars and reading countless books without seeing real results.

The turning point, a pivotal moment in my journey, came when my company was sold and I faced a significant pay cut. Although I was recruited to stay, I chose to leave, driven by a deeper desire for freedom and fulfillment.

Around this time, a mutual acquaintance connected me with the man who was to become my mentor, a renowned personal development coach, Bob Proctor. Bob asked me what I truly wanted, and I responded with a desire to create a life of freedom and the ability to do what I loved.

Despite my initial skepticism and past failures, I committed wholeheartedly to implementing discipline and overcoming doubts. In the first year of following Bob's mentorship, I experienced profound changes. I lost forty-two pounds, discovered my purpose in coaching, eliminated my debt, and earned a positive net of $282,000. Within two years, I was earning $1 million.

The key to this transformation was my discipline and commitment to doing exactly what Bob told me. Despite my initial doubts, I trusted the process and remained coachable. Motivation, which played a crucial role in my journey, came from being in a position where I had no choice but to perform. The sense of urgency propelled me to make significant changes.

Additionally, I continually raised my standards and pushed myself to achieve more and set higher goals. The mindset shift from merely achieving goals to making them a part of my identity played a crucial role in my success. Assisted by the power of mentorship, I learned to think big. My mentor taught me to expand my vision and set ambitious goals. My journey underscores the importance of having a mentor who can provide guidance, accountability, and critical feedback. Bob's mentorship helped me develop a winning mindset and adopt the habits necessary for sustained success.

Lead from the Heart

Leading with the heart has been a cornerstone of my success. I believe that true greatness and success come from the heart, where our deepest desires reside. By aligning my actions with my heart's desires and making irrevocable decisions, I have tapped into a limitless source of motivation and power.

I encourage you to remove scarcity from your heart and lead with an open heart so you can remove self-imposed ceilings and open up infinite possibilities. Self-image, understanding, and changing paradigms—which are a multitude of habits stored in the subconscious mind that shape our behaviors and results—was crucial for me. To change these paradigms, I employed repetition of new ideas and elite-level coaching.

Changing my self-image was essential to making lasting changes. By continually setting higher standards and goals, I ensured that my self-image evolved to support my aspirations. Creating a millionaire morning process—a structured morning routine—has been essential for setting the tone of the day. My daily processes include exercise, autosuggestion, gratitude practices, and meditation. This routine helps me start the day with positive intention and reinforces my goals and self-image.

Overcoming Challenges

Consistency in these practices builds momentum, which is critical for achieving and maintaining success. People often face the challenge of failing to change their identity and behaviors. Many people work hard but fail to see lasting results because they do not alter their self-image. True transformation requires changing identity-based behaviors, which can be achieved through continuous self-improvement practices and embracing failure as part of the learning process.

Reflecting on the early stages of my journey, I remember an overwhelming sense of fear and doubt. Leaving a stable six-figure job was daunting, especially with substantial debt. The security of a regular paycheck was hard to let go of, despite the dissatisfaction that accompanied it. However, my mentor's unwavering belief in my potential and the promise of a life aligned with my true desires gave me the courage to take that leap of faith.

When I began my mentorship, the first lesson was about the importance of daily habits. Bob emphasized that our daily actions define our future. He introduced me to *The Science of Getting Rich* by Wallace D. Wattles (which I have already mentioned). This book became my daily companion. Each morning I would read and copy passages from the book.

This practice wasn't just about understanding the content. It was about internalizing the principles and letting them shape my subconscious mind. The concept of thinking truth, regardless of appearances, was particularly challenging. It kept me focused on my desired outcomes, no matter what my current situation looked like.

Oh, yes, there were days when my financial situation seemed bleak and doubts crept in, but I learned to see these moments as tests of my commitment. By sustaining consistent thoughts on the truth, I prevented my mind from being swayed by negative appearances and stayed focused on my goals.

Being Consistent

The discipline of consistency became my mantra. My mentor taught me that missing one day of practice was understandable, but missing two days in a row was not an option. This rule instilled a level of discipline that was new to me. On days when my motivation was low, I reminded myself of my commitment and the long-term vision I was working toward. This unwavering discipline began to reflect in all areas of my life and helped me maintain a positive attitude.

The transformation in my attitude was profound. I realized that maintaining a positive attitude, especially during challenging times, was a powerful tool for personal growth and success. By adopting disciplined practices such as reading and writing inspirational passages daily, I internalized positive principles and transformed my mindset. This shift in attitude had a cascading effect on my actions and results.

Building Resilience

Building resilience through mental reinforcement became a cornerstone of my growth. Engaging in activities that strengthened positive thoughts, beliefs, and attitudes helped reprogram my subconscious mind. This wasn't overnight change, but a gradual process of replacing negative thought patterns with empowering ones. The consistency of these mental exercises fortified my mind, making it resilient to life's ups and downs. Neuroscience supports the idea that consistent mental reinforcement can reshape the brain.

The brain's plasticity allows it to form new neural pathways based on repeated experiences. By consistently engaging in positive mental practices, I created and strengthened neural pathways that supported resilience and positive thinking. This scientific backing reinforced my belief in the process and motivated me to keep going.

The challenge of maintaining focus on desired outcomes during adverse circumstances was one of the toughest challenges. Emotional turmoil, distraction, self-doubt, and external pressures often threatened to derail my progress. However, I learned to view these challenges as opportunities for growth. Each obstacle became a stepping stone, teaching me valuable lessons and strengthening my resolve for staying focused. To stay focused, I set clear and specific goals. This clarity provided a road map for where I wanted to go, making it easier to stay on track.

Practicing mindfulness and self-awareness helped me manage stress and recognize when I was becoming distracted or overwhelmed. Developing a support system of like-minded individuals provided encouragement and accountability and kept me motivated. A resilient mindset brought numerous benefits and enabled me to handle stress and maintain focus on my goals.

I improved my overall well-being by engaging in daily practices such as reading, writing, affirmations, visualization, and gratitude. I fortified my mental resilience. This mental fortitude allowed me to navigate challenges more effectively and stay focused on my goals.

The Power of Continued Growth

Adopting a standard of continued growth became a commitment to perpetual self-improvement in learning. This philosophy fostered resilience, adaptability, and a relentless pursuit of excellence. It meant prioritizing personal and professional development above comfort and complacency. Embracing a growth mindset involves seeing challenges as opportunities to learn and grow rather than as obstacles to avoid.

Setting clear, achievable goals that pushed me beyond my comfort zone was essential. Reflecting on my progress and areas for improvement allowed me to celebrate my achievements while identifying new areas to develop. I engaged in lifelong learning activities such as reading, taking courses, and attending workshops, which expanded my knowledge and skills and enhanced my overall growth.

Overcoming Barriers to Growth

The path to continuous growth was not without challenges. Fear of failure, lack of motivation, and comfort with the status quo often impeded progress. Overcoming these barriers required a strong commitment to my goals and a willingness to embrace discomfort as a natural part of the growth process. Cultivating a supportive environment of individuals who encouraged my growth provided the motivation and perspective needed to stay on track. Maintaining a standard of continued growth brought far-reaching professional benefits. It led to greater career opportunities, increased innovation, and enhanced problem-solving abilities.

My practice contributed to a richer, more fulfilling life, which improved relationships and gave me a deeper sense of purpose. Embracing this standard fostered resilience and helped me navigate life's challenges with confidence.

Leading by Example

Through my journey, I learned the importance of leading by example through sharing my experience and insights. I aim to inspire others to venture down their own path of personal development and growth. Mentorship played a crucial role in my success, so I sought to provide the same guidance and support to others. By committing to continuous growth and self-improvement, I created a ripple effect by influencing those around me to strive for their highest potential.

My journey from debt and dissatisfaction to success and fulfillment is a powerful example of the transformative power of personal development. By adopting disciplined practices, seeking mentorship, raising standards, and leading with the heart, anyone can remove the ceilings in their life and achieve extraordinary results.

My Story Can Be Your Story

My story is a testament to the potential that lies within each of us: to create a life of freedom and success by continually striving for personal growth and embracing the process of transformation, living authentically, embracing your human potential, and committing to continued growth and perpetual self-improvement and learning.

By setting high expectations for yourself, embracing a growth mindset, and integrating learning into your daily routine, you can achieve remarkable personal and professional development. Overcoming barriers to growth and cultivating a supportive environment further enhance your ability to maintain this standard.

Ultimately, the commitment to continued growth leads to a richer, more fulfilling life and empowers you to navigate challenges with resilience and confidence. Embrace these practices. Commit to consistency, and watch as your life begins to change for the better.

Words of Encouragement

Embarking on a transformative journey is both a courageous and rewarding endeavor. As you set out to remove the ceilings in your life and unlock your true potential, remember that every step you take, no matter how small, is a significant stride toward your goals.

Embrace the process with an open heart, and trust in your ability to create the life you desire. Believe in yourself. Your journey begins with a belief in your own potential. Understand that you have within you all the resources and abilities needed for greatness. The path to transformation is not always easy, but your commitment to growth and improvement will guide you through any challenges.

Stay committed to your goals. Consistency and discipline are the cornerstones of success. Stay committed to your goals, even when faced with setbacks or doubts. Each day, reinforce your intentions through positive actions with a focused mindset. Remember that true change happens gradually, through persistent effort and unwavering dedication. Embrace learning and growth in every experience. Every success or failure is an opportunity to learn and grow. Embrace these lessons with gratitude, and use them to fuel your progress. Stay curious, seek knowledge, and remain open to new ideas and perspectives.

Continual learning is essential for maintaining momentum on your transformative journey. Surround yourself with support. Surround yourself with people who uplift and inspire you. Seek out mentors, peers, and communities that share your vision for growth. Their support and encouragement can provide valuable insights, accountability, and motivation, and help you stay on track and reach new heights.

Lead with your heart. Your heart is your greatest guide. Let your deepest desires and passions lead the way and make decisions aligned with your true self. Tap into *you*. Tap into an inexhaustible source of strength and motivation, and you can overcome any obstacle and achieve your dreams. Visualize your success regularly. Visualize your goals as already achieved. This mental practice not only strengthens your belief in your abilities, but also aligns your actions with your aspirations. Visualization helps you stay focused, motivated, and connected to your vision of success.

Take bold, transformative action. Step out of your comfort zone. Take risks, trust in the process, and act on your ideas with confidence. Each bold step you take brings you closer to your goals and expands your horizons.

I leave you with these words: Your journey toward personal freedom and transformation is unique to you. Embrace it with enthusiasm and courage. Believe in your potential. Stay committed and

A Final Word: Step Into the Goal Achieved

continuously strive for growth. By doing so, you will not only remove the ceilings in your life but will also inspire others to embark on their own transformative journeys. Remember, the power to change your life lies within you. Take the first step today, and let your journey toward a life of freedom, success, and fulfillment begin.

Key Points in This Chapter

This book details the author's personal journey from being deeply in debt and unfulfilled in a corporate job to becoming a successful multimillionaire business owner and influential coach. His story is a testament to the transformative power of personal development and serves as an inspirational guide for you to unlock your full potential.

- Discover the power of self-identity, personal development, and disciplined action through books like *Think and Grow Rich* and *The Science of Getting Rich*.
- Find a transformative mentor and personal development coach.
- Develop a winning mindset by continually raising your standards, thinking big, and leading with the heart.
- Implement a structured morning routine and a consistent self-improvement practice to build momentum and achieve sustained success.
- Overcome common challenges such as fear, doubt, and lack of motivation by embracing a growth mindset and seeing obstacles as opportunities.
- Emphasize the importance of continued growth, lifelong learning, and leading by example to inspire others.

Acknowledgments

This book is not my work alone. It's the result of countless hours of reading and listening, countless conversations, hard earned lessons, and moments that have shaped me and my message to this point.

First, I want to thank God—Each idea, word and opportunity to serve others has been divinely inspired.

To my wife, Veronica—your love, patience, and belief in me are the greatest gift and source of strength. You are the single greatest decision of my life and a constant reminder of what unconditional love looks like. To Maya and Andre—you are my daily motivation, my greatest teachers and my greatest source of joy. Watching you grow keeps me grounded and reminds me what's important.

To my brother, Bobby—thank you for always being in my corner. Your loyalty and support have shaped so much of who I am and been an anchor through every season of my life.

To Mykie Stiller—my incredible business partner and dear friend. This book would not exist without your unwavering commitment to our mission. Thank you for pushing me, believing in me, and co-creating this movement with me.

To our world-class team at Voss Coaching Co—Thank you for your dedication, your energy, and your belief in helping others transform their lives. Every message, every event, every client success story is your success too.

To my mentor, Bob Proctor—for showing me what's possible and for shaping the way I think about life, success, and service. The lessons you poured into me continue to ripple out into thousands of lives every day.

To our clients—the men and women who have trusted us, challenged themselves, and done the work. You are living proof that transformation is not only possible—it's inevitable when you commit. Your courage fuels this mission.

And finally, to every person who picks up this book—I wrote this for you. May it awaken something within you, remind you of your potential, and call you to live with greater purpose, discipline, and freedom.

Here's to the work, the process, and the transformation that never ends.

—Arash Vossoughi

About the Author

Arash Vossoughi is a thought leader, coach, and entrepreneur who has dedicated his life to helping individuals unlock their potential and live in true freedom.

For over two decades, Arash has studied, applied, and taught the timeless principles of personal development. He has helped over 100,000 clients overcome limiting beliefs, rewire their self-image, and create lives filled with purpose, prosperity, and personal power.

As the cofounder and president of Voss Coaching Company, Arash leads with bold honesty, deep belief in human potential, and an unwavering commitment to helping people do the inner work required to live extraordinary lives.

His mission is simple but powerful: help people do the work and achieve freedom.

www.ingramcontent.com/pod-product-compliance
Lightning Source LLC
Chambersburg PA
CBHW072200070526
44585CB00015B/1227